30-SECOND
FEMINISM

30-SECOND FEMINISM

The 50 most fundamental concepts
in feminism, each explained in
half a minute

Editor
Jess McCabe

Contributors
Veronica I. Arreola
Laura Bates
Red Chidgey
Shannon Harvey
Os Keyes
Gillian Love
Nadia Mehdi
Chitra Nagarajan
Minna Salami
Sarah Tobias

Illustrations
Nicky Ackland-Snow

IVY PRESS

First published in the UK in 2019 by
Ivy Press
An imprint of The Quarto Group
The Old Brewery, 6 Blundell Street
London N7 9BH, United Kingdom
T (0)20 7700 6700 **F** (0)20 7700 8066
www.QuartoKnows.com

British Library Cataloguing-in-
Publication Data
A catalogue record for this
book is available from the
British Library.

ISBN: 978-1-78240-841-3

This book was conceived,
designed and produced by
Ivy Press
58 West Street, Brighton BN1 2RA, UK

Publisher **Susan Kelly**
Creative Director **Michael Whitehead**
Editorial Director **Tom Kitch**
Art Director **James Lawrence**
Project Editor **Caroline Earle**
Copy Editor **Katie Crous**
Designer **Ginny Zeal**
Picture Researcher **Sharon Dortenzio**
Illustrator **Nicky Ackland-Snow**
Glossaries **Katie Crous**

Printed in China

10 9 8 7 6 5 4 3 2 1

Cover images
Top left and right: Shutterstock/Everett Historical
Centre: Shutterstock/Jacob Lund
Bottom: Library of Congress, Washington D.C.

CONTENTS

INTRODUCTION

Jess McCabe

While editing the feminist magazine, *The F-Word*, I would receive submissions every day from young women who had just discovered feminism. To be more specific, they knew that feminism existed before and may have heard it talked about, not always in a positive light. But they had just discovered that feminism had something to say that was relevant to their own lives. One example was a school student who was being sexually harassed in class. Another was a woman who had been raped and was going through the court system. Very often it was young women who were trying, in the face of society's expectations, to find a way to feel good about their bodies, and, on a deeper level, about themselves.

At the time of writing, the most recent feminist explosion of activism has seen mostly women and girls using social media to tell thousands of individual stories of sexual harassment and violence, using hashtags like #MeToo and #MeuPrimeiroAssedio (#MyFirstHarassment). They have been flooding social media with so many of these stories that their perspective cannot be ignored anymore. This is one way to think about what feminism is: women describing their lives and using what they learn to change the world.

Feminism is made up of the familiar material of our everyday lives, yet it can seem difficult to understand. What are the most important feminist ideas? What do terms like 'patriarchy' and 'intersectionality' mean? How have they emerged from historical conditions facing women around the world – from a lack of basic rights to harassment and intimidation online? And how have activists and activism shaped those ideas? What follows is a concise introduction and starting point to answer some of these questions and demystify feminism.

A word about the structure of this book. It has been designed so you can flick through it and read about individual topics or people as they strike your fancy, rather than reading cover to cover. Each topic is covered in only 300 words, on one easy-to-understand page. We have striven to

use everyday language, not jargon. Each page is broken down even further into a 3-second nugget, to convey the main point, and more extended 30-second and 3-minute explanations from which you can learn more. It is organized into seven chapters, each of which introduces you to the main ideas of feminism and how those ideas came into being. In deciding what to include, I have tried to resist centring only on the experiences of white Western women, reflecting instead the true range of contributions to feminist thought and activism.

The first section, **Feminism on the Move**, is a brief history of the feminist movement up to the present day. There is no real 'beginning' to feminism – throughout history, individual women have been striving against different forms of sexism in their own ways. We have opened with this history primer because feminist ideas can never really be divorced from the historical context in which they arose. That is true of the first campaigns for women's property rights in Europe, when women could not own property, nor inherit, nor vote, nor end a marriage, nor gain custody of their children. It was true of the emergence of postcolonial feminism in response to the limitations of feminist activism in the 1970s. And it is true of today's online feminist activism, which has embraced the immediacy of social media to push women's stories into the mainstream like never before in history, with radical consequences.

The next chapter, **The Struggle for Equality**, considers in depth the struggle for basic rights and legal equality. This starts with the conceptualization of women as equal to men, which Mary Wollstonecraft set out in *The Vindication of the Rights of Woman*, the thread of this idea has led to voting rights, attempts to reach pay equality, improved workplace conditions, and changes in international and national law. This includes everything from the contributions of Anita Hill in the 1990s to exposing workplace sexual harassment, to the role of feminism in shaping independence movements. Of course, feminism is about so much more than achieving legal equality. For this reason, the next

chapter is called **The Personal is Political**. This was one of the rallying cries of the women's liberation movement in the 1960s and 1970s, and is a concept that still runs deep in feminist thought.

The next chapter is called **Against Patriarchy** and it introduces how feminist theory has unpacked the role of male supremacy in our society and culture, and the impact this has had on our lives. It is here we talk about violence against women, and how feminism has brought about an understanding of sexual and interpersonal violence as not just individual crimes, but as part of patriarchy oppression.

No book on feminism can neglect the important battleground of women's control over their own bodies. For that reason, **My Body, My Choice** goes into some depth on this issue, looking at abortion and choice, and beyond. Feminists have been hugely influential in shaping a rights- and justice-based approach to sex, sexuality, contraception and abortion during pregnancy and labour.

Next, in a chapter called **Sisterhood**, we turn to one of the major debates in feminism of the twentieth and twenty-first centuries: who is feminism for? Why does so much of the feminist activism that we hear most about seem to involve white, privileged, Western women?

Finally, to close the book, in **A Movement of Protest**, we look at some of the individual activists and movements that have defined feminism. What does activism look like? What has it achieved? What are some of the underlying principles of that activism?

This book will introduce you to the crucial theories and analyses of feminist thought, but this is just a beginning. We hope that this introduction will give you the inspiration to look further and learn more. Feminism has often been diminished and feminists ridiculed, suppressed and even imprisoned for their activism. However, feminist ideas have reached far and wide – changing economics, literature and art, and even challenging how scientific experiments are carried out and how buildings are designed. Feminism has changed the world – read on to find out how.

FEMINISM ON THE MOVE

FEMINISM ON THE MOVE
GLOSSARY

alt-right Right-wing, primarily online movement, based in the US, which favours extremist beliefs and white nationalism.

big three Feminist theory which argues that patriarchy, capitalism or socialization are the causes of women's oppression.

black feminism Aims to empower black women by focussing on how racism and sexism create social issues and inequalities.

bra-burner Contemptuous term for a militant feminist, or some one perceived as such, which derives from the occasional bra-burning protests of the 1960s.

call-out culture Chiefly online phenomenon of naming and shaming perceived perpetrators of bigotry, abuse or misconduct, including sexism.

cisgender People whose gender identity matches the gender of their birth.

e-bile Email conveying anger and revulsion.

feminist blogosphere Collection of blogs and bloggers considered to be feminist.

first-wave feminism Activity surrounding women's suffrage at the height of colonial domination. It set out to achieve rights for women and to redefine 'womanhood'.

fourth-wave feminism Twenty-first century resurgence in feminism associated with the use of social media.

gender mainstreaming Incorporation of a gender-equality perspective in public policies.

grassroots activism Actively campaigning to make a difference; relies on the basic rights to freedom of speech and expression.

hashtag politics Categorizing tweets by using politically orientated labels, or #, and thereby showing support for, or affiliation to, a political stance or movement.

herstory Term coined by activists in the 1970s to draw attention to how mainstream historians tended to ignore women's history.

liberal feminists Believe that gender stereotypes, unequal participation and discriminatory practices uphold inequality.

Marxist feminists Blame capitalism for women's oppression through its dependence on women's unpaid domestic labour and unequal participation in labour.

men's rights activists (MRAs) Explicitly anti-feminist male movement.

#MeToo Online campaign run by Tarana Burke since 2005 and used by women to share experiences of violence.

New Left Radical Western political movement of the 1960s and 1970s that campaigned for a broad range of social issues such as civil rights and feminism.

patriarchy The systematic dominance of men over women.

radical feminists Believe that the root of women's oppression is patriarchy.

Riot grrrls Collective name for women who were reacting to the male-dominated rock and punk music scenes, combining feminist analysis with DIY punk politics.

second-wave feminism Another way of referring to the women's liberation movement, which followed the 'first wave' (suffrage campaigns).

socialist feminism Offshoot from the New Left that arose in the 1960s–70s and focuses on the interconnectivity of patriarchy and capitalism.

state feminisms Feminism endorsed by the government of a state or nation.

suffrage The right to vote in political/ governmental elections.

third-wave feminism Vibrant movement of the 1990s that meshed autobiographical experience with cultural politics.

Third World feminism Originates from internal Third World ideologies and socio-cultural factors, rather than being imported from the West.

trolling (Internet) Using social media forums to provoke and sow discord by posting inflammatory and abusive messages.

the woman question Refers both to an intellectual debate from the 1400s to the 1700s on the nature of women and to feminist campaigns for social change after this time.

women of colour (WOC) Political term used to collectively describe females of colour; emerged in the violence against women movement and became a unifying term in the 1970s for all minority women experiencing marginalization, with race and ethnicity as a common factor.

SUFFRAGE & EARLY FEMINISM

30-second feminism

Imagine if you had no legal or political rights in the eyes of society. Your children's fate belonged solely in the hands of your husband, as did your body. You had no right to own property or participate equally in education or social life. You were considered childlike and irrational. You had no say in the workings of the State or in daily life, which were maintained by male authorities such as fathers, husbands, religious figures and man-made laws. The idea of you voting would provoke ridicule and violence. 'Feminism' was a term coined in France in 1895 in response to these conditions, and became a synonym for women's emancipation. From the mid 1860s women and their male allies organized collectively and persistently to fight for women's political, economic, social and cultural recognition and representation around the world. Women's suffrage marked a watershed struggle in this fight for gender equality. It is this groundswell of activity that is known as 'first-wave feminism'. This political wave, taking place at the height of colonial domination, set out to achieve not only rights for women, but also to challenge, deconstruct and, sometimes, re-emphasize society's ideas about femininity and womanhood.

3-SECOND SLAM
From the mid-nineteenth century, women organized political movements around the world to secure cultural, social, legal and economic rights for women.

3-MINUTE SPEECH
Global suffrage struggles stretched from the nineteenth to the twenty-first century. New Zealand was the first country to award equal suffrage in 1893. Australia followed in 1902, but only for white women; Aboriginal people could not vote until 1962. Azerbaijan awarded equal suffrage in 1918. The United States conceded in 1920; but African-Americans could not vote until 1965. In 2015, women in Saudi Arabia cast their votes for the first time.

RELATED TEXTS
See also
A VINDICATION OF THE RIGHTS OF WOMAN
page 44

SENECA FALLS
page 46

SUFFRAGE & ABOLITION
page 48

3-SECOND BIOGRAPHIES
EMMELINE PANKHURST
1858–1928
Led the Women's Social and Political Union and called for 'guerrilla warfare' against the British government following a 50-year struggle for the vote.

TANG QUNYING
1871–1937
Assumed leadership of the militant Women's Suffrage Alliance in the early years of the Republic in China.

30-SECOND TEXT
Red Chidgey

Women the world over used both militant and peaceful tactics to fight for their right to vote.

WOMEN'S LIBERATION MOVEMENT

30-second feminism

3-SECOND SLAM
The women's liberation movement called on governments to achieve equality for women and organized collectively to challenge women's everyday experiences of oppression.

3-MINUTE SPEECH
The WLM circulated ideas through feminist magazines, newspapers, books and art. They believed 'the personal is political'. This movement struck at the very heart of intimate life, as the everyday is the realm in which gendered expectations and experiences are made and remade. Women liberationists created their own media, political groups, businesses, family structures and ideas of what it meant to be a 'woman'. In doing so, they changed the landscape of gender politics.

From the unrest of the New Left and the civil rights movement, the women's liberation movement (WLM) emerged in the late 1960s and 1970s to bring gender politics centre-stage. Tired of hearing that the 'woman question' could wait until wider revolution and reform, feminists created their own autonomous movements. They were driven by a ferocious intellectual energy that refused to leave everyday gender relations unexamined – ranging from the politics of housework to the conditions of women in prison. For activists across Western Europe and North America, organizing was most effective when it was decentralized and collective. While each national women's movement came up with its own priorities and agendas, key demands included: equal pay, educational and job opportunities; free contraception and abortion on demand; legal and financial independence for all women; the right to a self-defined sexuality; and freedom from sexual violence and coercion. As an unfinished legacy, WLM demands from the late 1960s and 1970s continue to have a powerful resonance in today's era of gendered wage gaps, conservative attacks on abortion rights and the #MeToo movement against workplace sexual harassment and rape.

RELATED TEXTS
See also
CONSCIOUSNESS-RAISING
page 62

PATRIARCHY
page 80

WHOSE SISTERHOOD?
page 118

3-SECOND BIOGRAPHIES
ANTOINETTE FOUQUE
1936–2014
Co-founded the French women's liberation movement after the student protests of May 1968.

GERMAINE GREER
1939–
Australian writer and provocateur who became seen as the face of women's lib following her bestselling *The Female Eunuch*.

30-SECOND TEXT
Red Chidgey

Feminist activism has done much to help reshape public policies and attitudes.

WOMANISM

30-second feminism

3-SECOND SLAM
Womanism is a creative
and political call to
recognize the priorities
of black feminists and
to recentre the lived
experience and struggles
of women of colour.

3-MINUTE SPEECH
Black feminist scholars
have taken up and critiqued
womanism. Patricia Hill
Collins argues that
'womanism' speaks to the
experiences of African-
American women, while
the term 'black feminism'
speaks to women of colour
more globally. Clenora
Hudson-Weems puts
forward the idea of
Africana Womanism to
speak to all women of
African descent. In this
Afrocentric agenda, issues
of self-definition, struggling
with males against
oppression, black female
sisterhood, authenticity,
family and spirituality are
brought to the fore.

A black feminist or feminist of colour, serious and playful. A woman who loves other women, sexually or non-sexually. A woman committed to the well-being and survival of males *and* females, and to herself, unconditionally. Someone who loves music, dance, spirit and the struggle for justice. This is how Alice Walker coined the term 'womanism' in her essay collection *In Search of Our Mothers' Gardens* (1983). In response to racism in the women's liberation movement and the sexism of the Black Power movement, the 1970s and 1980s saw a surge in black feminist writing, creativity and art that centred the lived experience and political expression of women of colour. Walker drew on her talents as a writer to offer womanism as a vital and vivid new concept to express the inventiveness and courage needed to build a broad-based coalition, rooted in everyday black experience. She argued that womanism and feminism were interconnected, famously writing 'Womanist is to feminist as purple to lavender'.

RELATED TEXTS
See also
INTERSECTIONALITY
page 72

AUDRE LORDE
page 124

BLACK FEMINISM
page 126

3-SECOND BIOGRAPHIES
ALICE WALKER
1944–
Poet, writer, activist and
author of the award-winning
The Color Purple.

CLENORA HUDSON-WEEMS
1945–
Academic and author
of *Africana Womanism:
Reclaiming Ourselves*.

PATRICIA HILL COLLINS
1948–
Academic, activist and author
of *Black Feminist Thought*.

30-SECOND TEXT
Red Chidgey

Womanism is a reaction to feminism of white women, which was felt to have failed to represent all women.

THIRD WAVE
30-second feminism

3-SECOND SLAM
Among claims in the 1990s
that feminism was dead,
a vibrant new feminist
movement exploded that
meshed autobiographical
experience with
cultural politics.

3-MINUTE SPEECH
Feminist historians and
activists debate the
usefulness of the 'wave'
narrative. For some,
the metaphor creates
antagonistic divisions
based on age and glosses
over the complexities of
past struggles. For others,
the wave metaphor creates
a new vitality for feminist
politics and draws
attention to how
movements are shaped
by political, economic
and technological shifts.
Third-wave feminisms,
nonetheless, have been
critiqued for being too
individualistic and as
being mostly relevant to
Anglo-American women.

Feminist history has long been characterized as existing in peaks and troughs, with new feminist generations seeking to make connections and breaks with movements that came before. In the opening pages of the bestselling publication *The Female Eunuch*, written during the first years of women's liberation, Germaine Greer famously declared that the book was part of a 'feminist second wave'. The struggle for women's suffrage was reformist, Greer argued, while the new women's liberation movement was revolutionary. Second-wave feminisms peaked in the 1970s and started to dissipate in the 1980s, following shifts in the political and economic landscape and internal divisions within its own ranks. In the 1990s, the American media led the charge that feminism was dead and passé. Feminist activism needed to be revitalized. New activists emerged, calling themselves riot grrrls and Third-Wave Feminists. These activists used music and fanzines to tell personal stories of sexism, racism and homophobia. They called for an 'intersectional' politics that included women of colour. Third-wave feminists wanted a new kind of feminist activism that spoke to their experiences as young women and queer youth and that was grounded in the micro-politics of their everyday lives.

RELATED TEXTS
See also
WOMEN'S LIBERATION
MOVEMENT
page 18

INTERSECTIONALITY
page 72

RIOT GRRRL
page 144

3-SECOND BIOGRAPHIES
KATHLEEN HANNA
1968–
American singer, musician,
artist and feminist activist
who pioneered the riot grrrl
movement and writes for
punk zines.

REBECCA WALKER
1969–
American activist, and
daughter of Alice Walker, who
brought media attention to
the term 'third-wave feminism'
in 1992, when she wrote *Ms.*
magazine article 'Becoming
the Third Wave'.

30-SECOND TEXT
Red Chidgey

*Third-wave feminists
claimed a new kind
of sexual politics.*

FEMINISM IN INSTITUTIONS

30-second feminism

RELATED TEXTS
See also
FEMINISM & INTERNATIONAL
LAW
page 54

FEMINIST ECONOMICS
page 74

REFUGE MOVEMENT
page 82

3-SECOND SLAM
Feminists have a complex relation with state and social institutions, seeking change in legislation and policies, while agitating for transformations beyond them.

3-MINUTE SPEECH
The number of countries with a woman Head of State or Government increased from eight in 2005 to 17 in 2017, according to the Inter-Parliamentary Union. The number of women Members of Parliament across the globe stands at just over 23 per cent. The top five countries with the largest share of women ministers are Bulgaria, France, Nicaragua, Sweden and Canada, who boast over 50 per cent of women in ministerial positions.

From the beginning, and throughout the years of women's liberation and the third wave, a significant strand of women's rights activism looked to reform the way that various institutions are involved in sexism and oppression. Institutions – which includes organs of government and civil society, such as trade unions, universities, police forces and parliaments – can be gendered in multiple ways. In most parts of the world, institutions that play a significant role in shaping everyday life began as either excluding women or were run largely by men. Feminist interventions have not only been concerned with getting more women into positions of power, but have also interrogated the workings of institutional culture. For example, offensive humour operates as an exclusion strategy, alongside harassment and stereotyping. Following the successes of second-wave feminism, quotas, equality legislation and gender impact assessments have all been introduced. At the Fourth UN Women's Conference of Beijing in 1995, activists introduced 'gender mainstreaming', a gender-equality perspective for all public policies. Some feminists contest this process, particularly how gender equality is defined and how it can avoid reproducing the norms of institutions led by white heterosexual men.

3-SECOND BIOGRAPHIES
BENAZIR BHUTTO
1953–2007
Pakistani politician who was the first woman leader of a Muslim nation in modern history, serving as Prime Minister of Pakistan.

JACINDA ARDERN
1980–
New Zealand Prime Minister and the first world leader to bring an infant to the United Nations General Assembly.

30-SECOND TEXT
Red Chidgey

Feminism seeks to highlight and question patriarchy embedded in institutions.

STRANDS OF THEORETICAL FEMINISM

30-second feminism

Feminist academic theory has developed alongside activism: its purpose, to illuminate the reasons why gender inequalities persist and what can be done to shatter them. As women's studies became established in universities in the 1970s and 1980s in the West, feminist theory bloomed. Three main camps of thought emerged, called the 'big three'. These perspectives offered competing explanations for how to identify and transform sexist power relations. For radical feminists, the root of women's oppression is patriarchy – the systematic dominance of men over women. Women are viewed as a sexual class, with gender inequalities originating in social structures imposed upon women through their biology. The nuclear family, sexual violence and pornography are key concerns. Marxist feminists see a different structure underpinning gender oppression: capitalism. Capitalism depends upon women's unpaid domestic labour and unequal participation in the labour force. To overthrow gender injustice, capitalism must go. Liberal feminists refrain from identifying any overarching structure. Gender stereotypes, unequal participation in social life and discriminatory practices uphold inequities; a gradual process of democratic reform is needed to counteract this.

RELATED TEXTS
See also
POSTCOLONIAL FEMINISM
page 28

FROM PATRIARCHY TO
KYRIARCHY
page 92

QUEERING FEMINISM
page 130

3-SECOND SLAM
A 'big three' of feminist theory – based on radical, Marxist and liberal approaches – argues that patriarchy, capitalism or socialization are the causes of women's oppression.

3-MINUTE SPEECH
Feminist theory is constantly being debated. Some concepts (such as patriarchy) are now contested for being ahistorical and essentializing – not all men hold power over all women, and feminist theory must attend to injustices across gender, class, 'race', sexuality, religion, nation and dis/ability. The 'big three' of radical, Marxist and liberal perspectives are also not clear-cut. Socialist feminists, for example, see women's oppression as an effect of both patriarchy and capitalism.

3-SECOND BIOGRAPHIES
MARY WOLLSTONECRAFT
1759–97
Author of *A Vindication of the Rights of Woman*, a foundational text for liberal feminism.

FREDERICK ENGELS
1820–95
Penned *The Origin of the Family, Private Property and the State* in 1884 and argued that the origin of women's oppression evolved alongside the rise of class society.

30-SECOND TEXT
Red Chidgey

The 'big three' strands of thought refer to radical, Marxist and liberal feminist theory.

POSTCOLONIAL FEMINISM

30-second feminism

Postcolonial feminists critique

the long histories of global domination, colonialism and imperialism of European nations, to emphasize the continuing and violent legacies of these power formations from the fifteenth century to the present day. Colonial practices, such as establishing settler colonies or administrative dependencies in which indigenous populations are directly ruled or displaced, carry with them gendered, sexualized and racialized logics. Such ideologies include historical claims of 'civilizing' indigenous and colonized nations, or as scholar Gayatri Spivak puts it, 'the saving of brown women from brown men'. Postcolonial feminists are critical of Western feminisms and feminist theory. This includes how historical Western women's movements colluded with the ideological and material work of empire to advance their own concerns and rights, a primary example being the women's suffrage movement of the late nineteenth and early twentieth century. A postcolonial position is not just concerned with history, but also with how neo-colonial relations are made. The need for feminist postcolonial perspectives has been reinvigorated in recent years, in light of racist media and political discourse surrounding veiling, female genital mutilation, refugees and asylum seekers, and sexual trafficking.

3-SECOND SLAM
Postcolonial feminisms critique assumptions of 'the West' and 'the rest', and make clear the Euro–American bias of mainstream feminist theory and activism.

3-MINUTE SPEECH
Postcolonial feminisms have affinities with Third World feminism, aligned with colonized and low-income countries, and transnational feminisms, which consider feminist ideas and movements that circulate beyond the nation state. There has been a turn to decolonizing feminism more recently. This position calls for a feminism that is capable of re-thinking social justice and solidarity across 'race', gender, class, sexuality, nation and citizenship, and across the uneven power relations of the global North and the global South.

RELATED TEXTS
See also
WOMEN IN INDEPENDENCE MOVEMENTS
page 52

IMPERIAL FEMINISM
page 128

ABA WOMEN'S WAR
page 140

3-SECOND BIOGRAPHIES
GAYATRI SPIVAK
1942–
Argues that Western women falsely universalize women's oppression.

TRINH T. MINH-HA
1952–
Filmmaker who questions how to represent a Third World female 'other'.

CHANDRA TALPADE MOHANTY
1955–
Offers a decolonial approach that is anti-racist and anti-capitalist.

30-SECOND TEXT
Red Chidgey

By their very nature, colonial practices are unjust and exploitative.

FEMINIST MEMORY

30-second feminism

Activists in the 1970s coined the term 'herstory' to draw attention to how mainstream historians tended to ignore women's history. Feminist techniques of building historical resources include oral history interviewing, to capture the lives of women and other groups who have been historically marginalized from the written historical record. Building archives and new forms of historical knowledge have also been a key part of activist work. Alongside documenting women's forgotten history – or herstory – feminists also claim the importance of feminist memory. This is the imaginative and creative mobilization of women's pasts in order to imagine a better future. Between 1410 and 1414, the medieval author Christine de Pizan produced the illustrated manuscript, *The Book of the City of Ladies*. This set up a conversation between the author and three personified virtues: Reason, Rectitude and Justice. In the book, the virtues instruct de Pizan to build an allegorical city that can protect women – the walls and towers built from examples of female achievement across history. Featuring women's pasts as warriors, inventors, scholars, prophets, artists and saints, *The Book of the City of Ladies* emphasizes that remembering women's achievements is a key part of fighting for gender equality.

3-SECOND SLAM
Oppression works through erasing the histories and struggles of marginalized groups; to reclaim women's lives is a tactic of resistance.

3-MINUTE SPEECH
Feminist history and memory work are not just orientated to the past. Remembering women's histories can help to reclaim missing knowledge. Memory also creates imaginative and activist resources for the present and the future. Artists and writers have a special role to play in this memory work. They act as memory-keepers and generate stories that enable us to think differently about what women can do and what they can achieve.

RELATED TEXT
See also
WOMANISM
page 20

3-SECOND BIOGRAPHIES
SHEILA ROWBOTHAM
1943–
Socialist feminist historian and influential author who has documented how work and the family have shaped women's struggles.

MARUSYA BOCIURKIW
1958–
Ukrainian Canadian professor and artist who created 'The Laboratory of Feminist Memory', an online archive of feminist artefacts.

SISTERS UNCUT
2014–
Collective who use slogans and symbolism from first-wave feminists to direct media attention to economic cuts to domestic violence services under austerity.

30-SECOND TEXT
Red Chidgey

A medieval script depicted a city built from women's achievements, which also protects women.

THE RISE OF ONLINE FEMINISM

30-second feminism

At the turn of the twenty-first century, digital media has emerged as the most significant channel for organizing and campaigning to take place. Feminist blogs mostly replaced self-published magazines as central spaces in which feminists network and share ideas, and in turn blogs have largely been replaced by conversations on social media. 'Hashtag politics' have brought a new visibility to everyday experiences such as sexual assault. The Internet is a culturally ambivalent space: social media has facilitated a 'call-out culture' in which sexual harassment is made visible, sharable and challenged in the wake of the #MeToo movement, yet online platforms are largely unregulated spaces in which misogynistic trolling and harassment can escalate. Activists Laura Bates and Soraya Chemaly lobbied Facebook in 2013 to address user-generated content which promoted sexual and domestic violence; in a mile-stone response, the multi-national corporation agreed to update its guidelines and policy on hate speech and to improve training for its moderators. Online feminisms have proven crucial for organizing protest actions and campaigns internationally, such as the SlutWalk movement against sexual violence, and the Women's March against the inauguration of President Donald Trump.

3-SECOND SLAM
Digital technologies provide an expanded toolkit for feminist activism, yet also create a new cultural space for misogyny.

3-MINUTE SPEECH
The main advantage of online feminism is that it opens up new spaces for feminist discussions and campaigns, to extend beyond mainstream media gatekeepers and the limited reach of independent media. The disadvantage is that online feminisms are precariously positioned; they depend upon corporate-run platforms, such as Twitter and Facebook, to operate, while lobbying against such media giants for better governance on gender equality issues.

RELATED TEXTS
See also
EVERYDAY SEXISM
page 70

RAPE CULTURE
page 88

#FEMINISM
page 152

3-SECOND BIOGRAPHIES
SORAYA CHEMALY
fl. 2000–
Director of the Women's Media Center Speech Project and award-winning writer who advocates for safer online spaces for women.

TERESA SHOOK
fl. 2016–
Retired lawyer in Hawaii credited as the founder of the Women's March on Washington, first organized through Facebook following Donald Trump's election as the 45th President of the United States.

30-SECOND TEXT
Red Chidgey

Input from women's organizations is helping to shape the user guidelines of social media giants.

15 September 1977
Born in Enugu, Nigeria,
the fifth of six children,
to Grace Ifeoma and
James Nwoye Adichie

1995
Studies Medicine at the
University of Nigeria

1996
Immigrates to the United
States to study Political
Science at Drexel
University, Philadelphia

2005
First novel *Purple
Hibiscus* wins multiple
awards, including
a Commonwealth
Writers' Prize

2008
Earns a Master's degree
in African Studies from
Yale University

2015
In Sweden, every
16-year-old is given a
copy of Adichie's book
*We Should All Be
Feminists*, to encourage
gender equality

2017
After a friend asks for
parenting advice, Adichie
publishes *Dear Ijeawele,
or a Feminist Manifesto
in Fifteen Suggestions*,
outlining strategies to
empower children

CHIMAMANDA NGOZI ADICHIE

Chimamanda Ngozi Adichie has been hailed as a global icon for feminism and as a fresh-thinking public intellectual. She has written a number of prize-winning novels related to life in Nigeria and the United States, translated in over 30 languages, but it is her thinking on gender equality that has brought her to public attention.

Adichie grew up on a university campus in Nigeria, as her father was a professor of statistics and her mother an academic administrator. Education was an important value in her family and, as a high-performing student, Adichie was put on a scientific track. It was not until she moved to the United States to pursue her education that Adichie moved into the arts.

As she later recounts in media interviews, first- and second-wave feminisms never really appealed to her; this was not her story. She did not come to feminism through theory and books; she became a feminist as she grew up in Nigeria and observed 'an injustice that made no sense' in terms of how women were judged and treated as second-class citizens.

Her 2012 TED talk, and later-published book, *We Should All Be Feminists*, catapulted Adichie to the status of international feminist icon. Beyoncé famously sampled the talk in her single 'Flawless'. In 2017, Maria Grazia Chiuri, the artistic director of the luxury brand Dior, used the slogan 'We Should All be Feminists' on a T-shirt campaign, bringing this popular feminism into high fashion.

Adichie uses her platform to advocate for LGBT communities. Yet the novelist has been criticized by transgender communities following an interview with Channel 4 News in which she stated that she viewed trans women as 'trans women'; born with the privileges of men, she did not perceive trans women's experiences as the same as women who were born and raised female (also known as 'cis-gender' women).

In 2018, Adichie disclosed her experience of sexual harassment as a 17-year-old aspiring writer, assaulted by a senior media figure. Lending her support to the #MeToo movement during a keynote address to the Stockholm Forum for Gender Equality, Adichie continues to agitate for gender equality and to use her writing talents in order to challenge negative connotations of what a 'feminist' is and can be.

Red Chidgey

BACKLASH

30-second feminism

In 1991, the prize-winning
journalist Susan Faludi published a searing
account that gave name to a growing
phenomenon of anti-feminist sentiment.
Titled *Backlash: The Undeclared War Against
American Women*, Faludi surveyed popular
culture to reveal the extent of media-generated
myths about man shortages and barren
wombs – all drawing on unsubstantiated 'bad
science' to suggest that women were miserable
following the women's liberation movement.
But the concept of a backlash has outlasted
that moment in time, and become a generalized
concept used to describe how advances in
gender equality are met with rejection, hostility
and harassment. Recently this has included
attempts to revive traditional gender values and
to roll-back legislation on reproductive rights,
such as Polish law-makers' attempt to ban
abortion. The Internet has given credence to
neo-conservative and anti-feminist discourses,
subscribed to by men and women. In 2018, the
suspect of a deadly van attack in Toronto which
killed ten people wrote about an 'Incel Rebellion'
on Facebook, referring to an online community
of men who call themselves 'involuntarily
celibate', complaining they are not receiving
the sex they feel they are entitled to as men,
which translates into a strong hatred of women.

3-SECOND SLAM
Advances made by
women's movements
are met with virulent
backlashes, where
progressive legislation is
attacked and men position
themselves as the victims
of feminism.

3-MINUTE SPEECH
While men have long
served as allies to women
and are becoming more
comfortable in calling
themselves feminists,
men's rights activists
(MRAs) are explicitly
anti-feminist. Masculinity
scholars have noted a rise
in 'angry white males' in
the public sphere, claiming
victimhood. Recent
decades have also seen
the emergence of the
international Seduction
Community, a training
service for men in the art of
psychological manipulation,
based, problematically, on
turning a woman's 'no' in
to a sexual conquest.

RELATED TEXT
See also
THE POLITICS OF
MASCULINITY
page 90

3-SECOND BIOGRAPHY
SUSAN FALUDI
1959–
Prize-winning journalist and
author of *Backlash: The
Undeclared War Against
American Women* and
*Stiffed: The Betrayal of
the Modern Man*.

30-SECOND TEXT
Red Chidgey

*As feminists push
for greater equality,
some men push back
with a distinctly
anti-feminist stance.*

GLOBAL FEMINISM

30-second feminism

3-SECOND SLAM
Feminism started in most places in reaction to local issues, but has sought – with mixed success – to build a global movement.

3-MINUTE SPEECH
Some of the greatest feminist victories have been achieved when women joined forces globally. Organizations such as the Women's International League for Peace and Freedom (WILPF), the Convention on the Elimination of All Forms of Discrimination Against Women (CEDAW) – a crucial political instrument for feminist change that is, effectively, an international bill of rights for women – #1BillionRising and #MeToo are examples of the potential power in global feminist organizing.

Activists have always inspired and forged connections, for example, through antiracism and abolitionism. From this grassroots activism emerged the idea of a global feminism, linking how gender expression is experienced by people in different ways with a politics of solidarity. From early suffrage campaigning, activists sought to internationalize the movement, seeing gender oppression as a worldwide phenomenon. The constitution of the first International Congress on Women's Rights (ICW), in 1878, presented the organization as 'a federation of women of all races, nations, creeds and classes' – in theory. In practice, 'international' was more 'Western', and the ICW reproduced global power structures. However, by the end of the First World War, the ICW had added sections in Latin America, Asia, Africa and the Middle East. Then, as now, the 'we' of collective feminist identity was not a harmonious 'we', and unification was fraught with problems of imperialism and racism. Yet the war and the violence it inflicted upon women and children cemented the need for a global feminism that could collectively tackle patriarchy. Feminist international conferences, from the first International Feminist Congress in 1910 to the UN World Conferences on Women, have replicated the efforts –and problems – of the grassroots activists of the past.

RELATED TEXTS
See also
SUFFRAGE & EARLY FEMINISM
page 16

FEMINISM &
INTERNATIONAL LAW
page 54

LIBERIA WOMEN'S
MASS ACTION FOR PEACE
page 148

3-SECOND BIOGRAPHIES
WILPF
est. 1915
An international non-governmental organization that brings together women who are united in working for peace by non-violent means.

CEDAW
est. 1979
Crucial political instrument for feminist change that is, effectively, an international bill of rights for women.

30-SECOND TEXT
Minna Salami

Recognized as essential to tackling worldwide oppression, unity is capable of empowering the feminist movement.

THE STRUGGLE FOR EQUALITY

THE STRUGGLE FOR EQUALITY
GLOSSARY

abolitionist movement Aimed to end slavery, racial discrimination and segregation. Many suffrage activists became politically aware during the movement.

anti-apartheid Opposed to a policy or system of apartheid, such as the system of institutionalized racial segregation in South Africa from 1948 to the early 1990s.

colonization Settling among and establishing control over the indigenous people of an area; can take gendered forms, separating families, destroying communities and restricting women's power.

Civil War (US) Broke out in 1861, primarily as a result of the long-standing controversy over slavery, and was fought between the Union and Confederacy until the collapse of the latter in 1865.

Cold War Geopolitical tension, from 1947–1991, between the US and the Soviet Union, and both parties' allies, in the wake of colonialism's collapse after the Second World War.

Declaration of Sentiments Document signed in 1848 by 68 women and 32 men at the Seneca Falls Convention. Principal author Elizabeth Cady Stanton modelled it upon the US Declaration of Independence, calling for property, employment and voting rights for women.

Enlightenment Philosophical movement in Europe and, later, North America, during the late seventeenth and early eighteenth centuries, which developed concepts such as reason, liberty, tolerance and scientific method, which women argued should apply equally to both sexes.

French Revolution Violent and far-reaching social and political upheaval in France and its colonies from 1789–99, which saw the monarchy being overthrown. Under the Revolution's slogan 'liberté, égalité, fraternité', women also protested, and feminism in France was born.

gendered Playing a significant role in shaping everyday life by either excluding women or being dominated by men.

LGBTQI Umbrella term for the lesbian, gay, bisexual, transgender, questioning/queer, and intersex community.

Quakers Members of The Religious Society of Friends, founded in England in the seventeenth century; beliefs include the idea that God is present in every person.

salons (hosting) Gathering of people in the home of an inspiring host, for enlightening conversation and debate.

Seneca Falls The first women's rights convention in the USA, held on 19th–20th July, 1848, in Seneca Falls, New York. Organized by Elizabeth Cady Stanton, Lucretia Mott and Mary Ann M'Clintock, the convention resulted in the Declaration of Sentiments.

sexism Prejudice or discrimination based on sex or gender, especially against women and girls.

sexual assault Any physical, psychological and emotional violation in the form of a sexual act, inflicted on someone without their consent.

sexual harassment Any unwanted behaviour of a sexual nature that makes the victim feel distressed, intimidated or humiliated.

SOGIE Abbreviation combining sexual orientation, gender identity and gender expression that has become a reference term to describe the LGBTQI community.

suffragettes Members of militant women's organizations in the early twentieth century who fought for the right to vote in public elections; formed in the UK in 1903 and led by Emmeline Pankhurst. Tactics included marches, attacking policemen, setting fire to buildings, throwing bombs and hunger-striking when in prison. Famously, suffragette Emily Davison was killed when she ran out in front of the king's horse in the Derby of 1913.

suffragists Campaigned for women's right to vote by using peaceful, constitutional methods; formed in the UK in 1897 and led by Millicent Fawcett. Over time, the suffragists built up supporters in Parliament.

A VINDICATION OF THE RIGHTS OF WOMAN (1792)

30-second feminism

3-SECOND SLAM
In one of the first written texts on women's rights, Wollstonecraft writes about women's oppression and argues that true freedom requires the education of women.

3-MINUTE SPEECH
Reviewed favourably by leading publications of the day, published in France and the US and cited by other writers, Wollstonecraft and her work became discredited after her death. Her husband published a biography of her life which caused shock by revealing suicide attempts and sex outside marriage, considered deplorable in a woman. Her ideas and work became tainted, although they continued to inspire. The suffrage movement reclaimed her memory and work from the 1870s onwards.

The Age of Enlightenment

dominated eighteenth-century Europe, with discussion on reason and science, liberty, progress, constitutional government and tolerance. Many women participated in debates, hosted salons, ran coffeehouses, joined debating societies and wrote texts. One of these women was Mary Wollstonecraft, who challenged notions that women were subordinate to and should obey men. *A Vindication of the Rights of Woman* builds on her earlier *A Vindication of the Rights of Men*, which argued that rights are based on justice not tradition, and responds to those who do not believe that women should be educated. She writes that women are not property traded in marriage but humans deserving of rights and education, and capable of rational thought but taught to be attractive and meek. Exposing double standards, Wollstonecraft demands responsibility for chastity be shared and calls on men to be modest. Described as a feminist philosopher, Wollstonecraft would not have called herself as such (feminism became a term only in the 1890s). Her insistence that women should be rational, her focus on morality, her praise for middle-class modesty and industry, and her advocacy for class distinction in education have also been critiqued.

RELATED TEXTS
See also
SUFFRAGE & EARLY FEMINISM
page 16

FEMINIST MEMORY
page 30

PATRIARCHY
page 80

3-SECOND BIOGRAPHIES
OLYMPE DE GOUGES
1748–93
French playwright who asserted women had the ability to reason and should benefit from the French Revolution.

PHILLIS WHEATLEY
1753–84
African poet, enslaved as a young woman, who examined enslavement and colonialism.

MARY WOLLSTONECRAFT
1759–97
English writer and philosopher who advocated women's rights and promoted republicanism.

30-SECOND TEXT
Chitra Nagarajan

Forward-thinking feminist philosophers emerged in the Enlightenment.

SENECA FALLS

30-second feminism

3-SECOND SLAM
The first women's rights convention in the USA was held on 19th–20th July, 1848, in Seneca Falls, New York.

3-MINUTE SPEECH
Seneca Falls was the catalyst for the US women's rights movement. It took 72 years from Seneca Falls to the ratification of the 19th Amendment of the US Constitution, which granted women the right to vote. During that time, the women's rights movement grew with each win, such as inheritance rights, as well as with each controversy, such as racism, which siloed women of colour.

Seneca Falls is considered the first major convening of women's rights leaders and activists in US history. The women who gathered had been campaigning for the right of women to own property and pursue education, and they were joined by active leaders in the abolitionist movement, who had been excluded from leadership conversations in the movement. This exclusion led many women to take the initiative in strengthening their organizations, and after years of gathering in each other's homes, Elizabeth Cady Stanton, Lucretia Mott and Mary Ann M'Clintock arranged a convention in Seneca Falls, New York, in July 1848. Hundreds of people attended to discuss a series of issues related to moving women closer to obtaining new political, social and civil rights. At the conclusion of the convention, 100 people signed the Declaration of Sentiments, modelled on the Declaration of Independence, which called for property, employment and voting rights, to name just a few. The issue of suffrage, or the right to vote, was almost left out of the Sentiments. The tension between radical women's rights activists, who wanted the right to vote, and those who sought a more incremental path towards equality was as present then as it is today.

RELATED TEXTS
See also
SUFFRAGE & EARLY FEMINISM
page 16

SUFFRAGE & ABOLITION
page 48

3-SECOND BIOGRAPHIES
LUCRETIA MOTT
1793–1880
Abolitionist who contributed to initiating the women's rights movement and planning the Seneca Falls conference.

MARY ANN M'CLINTOCK
1800–84
Co-founded the Philadelphia Female Anti-Slavery Society with Lucretia Mott and organized the first women's rights convention.

ELIZABETH CADY STANTON
1815–1902
Organized the first women's rights conventions in the US; leader in the early years of the suffrage movement.

30-SECOND TEXT
Veronica I. Arreola

Years of hosting salons galvanized women and led to the organization of seminal conventions.

SUFFRAGE & ABOLITION

30-second feminism

3-SECOND SLAM
What should have been a collaborative relationship between the anti-slavery movement, or abolitionists, and the women's right to vote movement, or suffragists, was tainted by the sexism and racism of the respective movements.

3-MINUTE SPEECH
The abolitionist and suffragist movements sought to correct the error the founding fathers made in leaving white women and all people of colour out of the US Constitution. While they fought for rights, they also battled sexism, classism and racism within their own ranks, which still reverberate in today's liberation movements.

Abolitionism, or the movement to end human slavery, was already in full force around the world as the fledgling United States established itself. The global movement inspired the American abolitionist movement, which was led by Quakers, Enlightenment thinkers and progressive Christians such as Angelina and Sarah Grimké. Yet the Grimkés and other leaders were often side-lined due to being women. This led to women organizing under their own flag instead of maintaining a universal suffrage movement. It is often thought that this move was purely a fight for women's right to vote, but it also encompassed pushing for laws that recognized women's ability to inherit property and money from their husbands, greater access to education and much more. In the pre-Civil War years, suffragists worked in collaboration with the abolitionist movement. American abolitionists such as Fredrick Douglass strategized with suffragist leaders, including Elizabeth Cady Stanton. When it was clear that universal suffrage would not be obtained in America, Stanton's faction of the suffrage movement resorted to racist logic in a failed attempt to win women the right to vote before enslaved men. The tension between sexism and racism continues throughout the modern-day civil rights and feminist movements.

RELATED TEXTS
See also
WOMANISM
page 20

SENECA FALLS
page 46

BLACK FEMINISM
page 126

3-SECOND BIOGRAPHIES
SARAH & ANGELINA GRIMKÉ
1792–1873 & 1805–79
Sisters and leaders in the abolitionist and women's rights movements.

SOJOURNER TRUTH
1795–1883
Escaped slavery and was an early critic of the suffrage movement's focus on white women's issues.

FREDRICK DOUGLASS
1818–95
Great orator within the abolitionist and suffrage movements.

30-SECOND TEXT
Veronica I. Arreola

Campaigners for suffrage and abolition initially joined forces, but the unity did not last.

30 July 1956
Born in Oklahoma

1977
Receives BA with honours
in psychology from
Oklahoma State
University

1980
Graduates from Yale Law
School with honours, is
admitted to the District
of Columbia Bar and
starts working at the law
firm of Wald, Harkrader
& Ross

1981
Becomes Attorney-
Adviser to Clarence
Thomas at the
US Department of
Education's Office for
Civil Rights and works
with him until 1983

1986
Joins University of
Oklahoma College of Law
to teach contracts and
commercial law

1989
Becomes the University
of Oklahoma College of
Law's first tenured black
professor

1991
Gives evidence in
televised hearings
that Clarence Thomas,
nominated to join the
Supreme Court, sexually
harassed her when he
was her supervisor

1995
Publishes *Race, Gender
and Power in America:
The Legacy of the
Hill-Thomas Headings*,
co-edited with Emma
Coleman Jordan

1997
Joins the Brandeis
University Women's
Studies Program

2017
Leads the Commission on
Sexual Harassment and
Advancing Equality in
the Workplace against
sexual harassment in the
entertainment industry

2018
Writes in the *New York
Times* offering advice
on the Supreme Court
nomination process for
Brett Kavanaugh, accused
of sexual assault by
Christine Blasey Ford

ANITA HILL

Born the youngest of 13 children and raised on her parents' farm, Anita Hill studied psychology before gaining her law degree. She worked for Clarence Thomas at the US Department of Civil Rights and Equal Employment Opportunity Commission from 1981 to 1983.

Clarence Thomas's confirmation to the US Supreme Court seemed certain until Hill's interview to the FBI talking about his sexual harassment was leaked. Hill testified in televised hearings with millions watching, saying Thomas repeatedly asked her out on dates, described pornography and boasted of his sexual prowess and penis length. Thomas denied all accusations, saying the hearing was a 'high-tech lynching for uppity black who in any way deign to think for themselves'.

The hearings divided the US over race, gender and politics. An all-white male committee asked ill-informed questions. Other women, waiting to speak of their own sexual harassment by Thomas, were not called to testify. Senators tried to discredit Hill with public campaigning, saying she was delusional, mentally unstable or exaggerating. Hill's credibility and reputation were put on trial, with one commentator describing her as 'a little bit nutty and a little slutty'. She received harassing phone calls and bomb and rape threats. In subsequent years, the University of Oklahoma defunded a professorship established in her name and officials tried to revoke her tenure.

Thomas's nomination was confirmed, but the repercussions of Hill's testimony reverberated through culture and politics. She had shone a light on workplace sexual harassment, which many women experienced but which was rarely publicly discussed, leading to growing consensus that sexual harassment is wrong. A month afterwards, Congress passed a law giving survivors the right to seek damages, back pay and reinstatement. A year later, complaints had increased by 50 per cent. Companies started anti-harassment training for employees. A record number of women were elected to legislatures in 1992, in what became known as the 'Year of the Woman'.

Since 1997, Hill has been part of the faculty of Brandeis University, where she is now a Professor of Social Policy, Law and Women's, Gender and Sexuality studies. She has spoken and written on race, women's rights and sexual harassment and co-edited a book examining the legacy of the hearings. Reflecting back in 2017, she said, 'We cannot underestimate the impact that those hearings had, even though the vote did not go the way most of us wanted.'

Chitra Nagarajan

WOMEN IN INDEPENDENCE MOVEMENTS

30-second feminism

3-SECOND SLAM
Women fight for self-determination, justice and rights, but are often marginalized, mocked and forgotten once that freedom is won.

3-MINUTE SPEECH
Across countries, male comrades tell women freedom fighters to prioritize independence then focus on women's rights. Often, that time never comes. Many postcolonial nations continue to be dominated by men. Women are not only erased from histories of the movement but also held to higher standards. Winnie Madikizela-Mandela, a leader of South Africa's liberation struggle, is forgotten, reduced to her husband or marred by allegations of violence – not the case for male anti-apartheid activists.

Colonization takes gendered

forms, separating families, destroying communities and restricting women's power. Worldwide, women have been integral to fighting against colonization and for independence through violent *and* peaceful means. Leaders such as Lakshmibai, Nanny and Nzinga in present-day India, Jamaica and Angola are known. But the names of countless other women who fought colonization, such as those of the Haitian Revolution, a slave uprising that led to independence, have been lost. Historical records, often by colonizing forces, are not only biased but tend to write out women. Women also played important roles in more recent independence movements. Hindi periodicals in early twentieth-century India, written by and for women and girls, discussed the role of women, social reform and home rule, shaped nationalist thought and instigated change. Hannah Cudjoe, Ama Nkrumah and Mabel Dove Danquah were some of the women who mobilized people, organized protests, spoke at rallies and wrote on the need for independence in Ghana. Mariana Grajales Cuello, today known as the Mother of Cuba, was one of many Afro-Cuban women who helped lead the fight against Spanish rule in Cuba. These women fought for freedom for their communities and for women.

RELATED TEXTS
See also
FEMINIST MEMORY
page 30

ABA WOMEN'S WAR
page 140

3-SECOND BIOGRAPHIES
TRU'NG TRẮC & TRU'NG NHỊ
fl. c. 12–43 CE
Vietnamese sisters who led the first independence movement against Chinese rule.

NEHANDA NYAKASIKANA
c. 1840–98
One of the leaders of Zimbabwe's first war of independence.

MARY THOMAS
c. 1848–1905
Alongside Agnes Salomon and Mathilda McBean, led the Fireburn plantation worker revolt and uprising against Danish colonialism in St Croix.

30-SECOND TEXT
Chitra Nagarajan

Alongside childcare and other family demands, women have fought successfully for independence.

FEMINISM & INTERNATIONAL LAW

30-second feminism

Feminist perspectives have

informed international law development since the early twentieth century. Better protections for civilians in conflict, anti-trafficking treaties and agreement that countries should settle disagreement peacefully were results of women's movements, as well as war's horrors. Yet, 'women's issues' were marginalized: law focused on protecting women, not recognizing rights. Feminist activists changed this. In 1979, the UN General Assembly adopted the Convention to Eliminate All Forms of Discrimination Against Women. In 1993, women's rights were recognized as human rights. In 2001, due to pressure from conflict-affected women worldwide, the UN Security Council adopted Resolution 1325 on women, peace and security, urging countries to increase women's participation in peace processes, integrate gender perspectives into policies and protect women and girls from violence. The Maputo Protocol recognized the right to abortion in 2003. In recent years, alliances between fundamentalist forces mean that activists have fought to ensure that gains made – especially on women's sexual and reproductive rights, early and forced marriage, and rights around sexual orientation, gender identity and expression (SOGIE) – are not reversed.

3-SECOND SLAM
International law starts to move from protecting countries and their rulers to protecting people (including women), largely due to feminism.

3-MINUTE SPEECH
Activists also bring feminist analysis into international law and policy not specific to women's rights. For example, the Convention on the Rights of Persons with Disabilities recognizes that women and girls with disabilities are subject to multiple discrimination and requires countries to act to ensure their human rights, while the Yogyakarta Principles on SOGIE talk of the need to combat gender stereotypes, prejudices and customs. Gender is slowly being mainstreamed across existing and developing international law.

RELATED TEXTS
See also
FEMINISM IN INSTITUTIONS
page 24

BACKLASH
page 36

WOMEN IN INDEPENDENCE
MOVEMENTS
page 52

3-SECOND BIOGRAPHIES
VIJAYA LAKSHMI PANDIT
1900–90
Imprisoned during India's independence struggle, she championed African and Asian self-determination and women's rights; first woman president of the UN General Assembly.

CHRISTINE CHINKIN
1949–
Leading legal thinker who was one of the pioneers of feminist critiques of international law before serving on UN human rights panels and missions.

30-SECOND TEXT
Chitra Nagarajan

Feminist activists have fought for women's rights to be recognized and upheld.

THE PERSONAL IS POLITICAL

THE PERSONAL IS POLITICAL
GLOSSARY

body positivity Modern feminist movement that fosters notions of self-love and acceptance, as well as the right for women to make choices about their own bodies.

consciousness-raising The sharing of stories about women's lives and their experiences of sexual harassment, rape, abortion, domestic violence and sexist comments and stereotypes.

dehumanization Portraying a person or group of people as objects or creatures, as 'less' than the rest of humanity; can serve to demonize the enemy, leading to increased violence, human rights violations and war crimes.

double discrimination Prejudice against a person for two of their characteristics, such as sexism intermingled with racism, homophobia or ageism. An example is saying that Asian women treat their men well by cooking and cleaning for them.

everyday sexism Women's experiences of sexism and sexual harassment in their daily lives. The Everyday Sexism Project is an online collection of such testimonies, to raise awareness of the scale and reality of the problem of gender inequality.

feminist economics Pioneers alternative economic models, taking a broader, gendered perspective of social and economic contexts.

feminization of labour The increasing integration of women into the labour market as a result of industrialization and globalization.

gender disaggregation Where macroeconomic variables are studied by gender, to reveal, for example, how the feminization of labour stimulates investment.

gendered Playing a significant role in shaping everyday life by either excluding women or being dominated by men.

honour killing Murder of a person (usually a woman) accused of bringing shame upon their family and/or community, committed by those (usually a family collective) who perceive they are defending their reputation; often a result of strongly misogynistic views towards women.

intersectionality The multiple and intersecting forms of oppression faced by black women and others.

labiaplasty Plastic surgery procedure to reduce the size of the labia minora or labia majora due to physical discomfort or aesthetic dissatisfaction.

LGBTQI Umbrella term for the lesbian, gay, bisexual, transgender, questioning/queer, and intersex community.

#MeToo Online campaign run by Tarana Burke since 2005 and used by women to share experiences of violence.

objectification Occurs when people (usually women) are dehumanized to the extent that they are treated like objects instead of human beings.

othering Viewing or treating a group of people or person as intrinsically different to the normative or favoured group, or the self. Largely driven by politicians and the media.

Playboy Bunny Specially selected and trained waitress at a Playboy Club (mainly between 1960 and 1988), who wore a special 'bunny suit' uniform.

politicize To make something political or to make someone politically aware.

second-wave feminism Another way of referring to the women's liberation movement, which followed the 'first wave' (suffrage campaigns).

sexual harassment Any unwanted behaviour of a sexual nature that makes the victim feel distressed, intimidated or humiliated.

sexualize To attribute sexual characteristics or qualities to something or someone, or to become aware of sexuality.

speak-out Event in which people publicly share their experiences of or views on an issue.

Women's Budget Group UK-based, independent, not-for-profit organization that monitors the impact of government policies on men and women.

THE FEMININE MYSTIQUE (1963)

30-second feminism

Focusing on the lives of relatively privileged, white, suburban women, *The Feminine Mystique* railed against 'the problem that has no name': the unhappiness and lack of fulfilment among American housewives. Friedan wrote: 'The women who suffer this problem have a hunger that food cannot fill ... We can no longer ignore that voice within women that says: "I want something more than my husband and my children and my home."' By suggesting that the frustration and malaise of millions of American women was a collective rather than an individual issue, Friedan tapped into the idea that the personal is political, a concept widely associated with second-wave feminism. Friedan argued that women, like men, required deeper fulfilment than simply being good spouses and homemakers, and that the notion that these were the ultimate pinnacles of female achievement was damaging to women, suffocating them and erasing their individual identities. She called this myth the 'feminine mystique', a phenomenon she blamed in part on male-dominated media (including women's magazines and advertising) and a sexist education system. Friedan advocated better education and meaningful employment as potential avenues for escape from the feminine mystique.

3-SECOND SLAM
Published in 1963, Betty Friedan's book *The Feminine Mystique* was one of the initial drivers of second-wave feminism in the US.

3-MINUTE SPEECH
The Feminine Mystique has been criticized for erasing the realities of women of colour and working-class women, many of whom already worked outside the home. As the feminist bell hooks later pointed out, black women often saw the labour associated with motherhood as a humanizing alternative to the alienation of paid work, rejecting the notion that motherhood was stifling. Critics noted that the book was homophobic: Friedan coined the term 'lavender menace' to refer to lesbians.

RELATED TEXTS
See also
CONSCIOUSNESS-RAISING
page 62

LAVENDER MENACE
page 120

3-SECOND BIOGRAPHIES
PAULI MURRAY
1910–85
Civil rights activist, lawyer, Episcopal priest, author and co-founder of the National Organization for Women (NOW), an organization created to fight workplace discrimination and other forms of gender inequality.

BETTY FRIEDAN
1921–2006
Writer, feminist activist and first president of NOW.

30-SECOND TEXT
Laura Bates

Friedan's mystique is the antithesis to the saying 'a woman's place is in the home'.

CONSCIOUSNESS-RAISING

30-second feminism

In the 1960s and 1970s, women started to meet in groups to share stories about their lives and their experiences of sexual harassment, rape, abortion, domestic violence and sexist comments and stereotypes. This activity came to be known as 'consciousness-raising', or CR – described by activists of the day as a tool to make sense of these experiences, not just as events that happened to individual women, but as part of a wider, systemic gender inequality. Or, in the language used at the time, 'the personal is political'. Consciousness-raising has the potential to spur change by creating awareness of inequalities that have previously been accepted. As women can experience misogynistic gender stereotypes and sexual harassment from childhood, they can think of these experiences as acceptable – even inevitable. Those who do object are often cast as overreacting, unreasonable or unnatural. So, consciousness-raising is a vital tool to enable women to realize, 'I am not alone', 'This is not normal', 'I do not have to put up with this', 'It is not my fault'. Modern feminists have turned to social media to facilitate a digital form of consciousness-raising, using platforms such as Twitter and tools such as hashtags to spread awareness quickly and effectively beyond self-selecting groups.

3-SECOND SLAM
Consciousness-raising is associated with second-wave feminism, particularly in the US, where women met in groups to discuss their lives and experiences of sexism.

3-MINUTE SPEECH
The #MeToo movement, started by activist Tarana Burke, and the Everyday Sexism Project are recent examples of this phenomenon, which have seen millions of women publicly share experiences of oppression and abuse. As well as empowering many women to report sexual violence or discrimination for the first time, these movements have started to create a cultural shift, sparking wider awareness of the problem and action to tackle it.

RELATED TEXTS
See also
THE RISE OF ONLINE FEMINISM
page 32

MOVEMENT TACTICS
page 138

#FEMINISM
page 152

3-SECOND BIOGRAPHIES
KATHIE SARACHILD
1943–
American writer and radical feminist who played a leading role in the consciousness-raising movement of the 1960s–70s.

ANNE FORER PYNE
1945–2018
Feminist activist and writer who coined the term 'consciousness-raising'.

30-SECOND TEXT
Laura Bates

The global reach of the Internet provides a useful CR platform that has popularized some feminist campaigns.

OBJECTIFICATION

30-second feminism

3-SECOND SLAM
As the name suggests, objectification occurs when people (usually women) are dehumanized to the extent that they are treated like objects instead of human beings.

3-MINUTE SPEECH
The objectification of women and its impact are wide-ranging: for example, the idea that a woman may be reduced to a mere object in which the honour of a family may reside, a concept which enables gender-based violence and 'honour killings'. The objectification of female politicians has been used worldwide to undermine their careers; for example, when political critics of Hillary Clinton distributed badges reading: 'KFC Hillary Special: 2 fat thighs, 2 small breasts, 1 left wing'.

Feminists coined the term objectification to describe how portrayals of women as objects have contributed to the denigration of women in society. This portrayal might be literal (an advert using a woman's body in place of a table) or more subtle (using parts of women's bodies, such as legs or breasts, to advertise unrelated products). Objectification is closely related to the idea that women are sexual possessions, available for male ownership, and that their bodies are fair game for comment, harassment and assault. Other forms of prejudice can compound objectification: LGBTQI women, for example, may be fetishized and stereotyped by others. Examples in pop culture include a photograph of Roman Abramovich's partner, Dasha Zhukova, sitting on a chair resembling a semi-nude, bondaged black woman, and the use of black women's bodies as sexualized props in the music videos of white pop stars. Feminists argue that the objectification of women contributes to their wider oppression by repeatedly and constantly showing women without voice or agency, reducing the scope of their participation in public life, creating a patriarchal hierarchy in which they are subjugated to men and undermining their individuality and achievements.

RELATED TEXTS
See also
PATRIARCHY
page 80

RAPE CULTURE
page 88

3-SECOND BIOGRAPHY
LUCY-ANNE HOLMES
1976–
British feminist activist and author, founder of the No More Page 3 Campaign, which successfully persuaded *The Sun* newspaper to stop publishing topless photographs of women.

30-SECOND TEXT
Laura Bates

Objectification sees women as sexual possessions, with physical assets usable as marketing tools.

BODY POSITIVITY

30-second feminism

3-SECOND SLAM
The body positivity movement aims to counter the criticism and policing of women's bodies in a sexist and patriarchal society.

3-MINUTE SPEECH
Some feminists have criticized the body positivity movement, suggesting that by merely focusing on expanding the definition of what is considered beautiful, it fails to dismantle the broader problem of women's value being reduced to their bodies and social perception of their attractiveness. Others have criticized the commercialization of the movement, with major brands using 'body positive' campaigns to reinforce the capitalist imperative for women to buy beauty products and toiletries.

The nineteenth-century Victorian dress reform movement campaigned against pressure for women to modify their bodies using tight corsets, arguing that women's physical comfort and freedom were more important. This was followed by the fat acceptance movement in the 1960s, which fed into today's body positivity movement. For feminists, the idea that women's bodies should conform to one, narrow, media-defined ideal, and valued accordingly, is part of the wider disenfranchisement of women. Body positivity is about self-love and acceptance, but also women's right to make choices about their own bodies. It also focuses on the intersections between sexism and other forms of inequality, seeking to redress the ways in which non-white, LGBTQI and disabled bodies are othered, erased and devalued within popular culture. Some have criticized the movement, suggesting that it privileges the voices and images of white and lighter-skinned women, despite the fact that black women have been navigating and promoting notions of body positivity for centuries; particularly given the othering and colonization of their bodies, and racist Western beauty standards. Some body positive movements seek to combat this, promoting 'visibility for all humans'.

RELATED TEXT
See also
THE RISE OF ONLINE FEMINISM
page 32

3-SECOND BIOGRAPHIES
MAMA CAX
1989–
Haitian–American amputee blogger, advocate and model.

HARNAAM KAUR
1990–
Bearded female British model, anti-bullying campaigner and body positivity activist.

SONYA RENEE TAYLOR
fl. 2004–
Author, poet, social justice activist and founder of The Body Is Not An Apology movement.

30-SECOND TEXT
Laura Bates

The Body is Not an Apology seeks to represent all sizes, genders, ages, abilities and ethnicities.

25 March 1934
Born in Toledo, Ohio

1944
Steinem's parents
separate, leaving her
to care for her mother

1956
Graduates Smith College

1963
Goes undercover at the
Playboy Club to expose
the conditions of
working women

1968
Co-founds *New York
Magazine*

1971
Co-founds *Ms. Magazine*
and the National
Women's Political Caucus

1983
Publishes *Outrageous
Acts and Everyday
Rebellions*

2005
Co-founds the Women's
Media Center

2013
Awarded the Presidential
Medal of Freedom by
Barack Obama

2015
Publishes *My Life on
the Road*

GLORIA STEINEM

Gloria Steinem had an unusual childhood. Her family lived an itinerant lifestyle, spending years on the road with her travelling-salesperson father. When her parents separated in 1944, it marked the beginning of a long period of caregiving, as Steinem looked after her mother, Ruth, who suffered from mental illness. It was, in part, Ruth's experiences at the hands of dismissive doctors and unsupportive employers that helped to spark Steinem's awareness of social injustice.

In the 1960s, Steinem started working as a journalist, covering issues such as contraception and women's careers. A 1963 article about the conditions and mistreatment of women working at the New York Playboy Club saw her go undercover as a so-called Bunny, resulting in a short period during which Steinem was unable to find employment because she was belittled and stigmatized as a result of stereotypes associated with women in that work. She said: 'I had now become a Bunny – and it didn't matter why.'

After attending an abortion 'speak out' (a sharing of testimonies to bust stigma) organized by a radical feminist group, Steinem found herself becoming increasingly active in feminist organizing and campaigning. She co-founded *New York Magazine*, for which she was a political columnist, and the feminist *Ms. Magazine*, which she edited for 15 years. She also co-founded many groups and organizations that fought for women's rights, many of them continuing to this day, including the Women's Media Center, the Women's Action Alliance, the National Women's Political Caucus, Voters for Choice and the Ms. Foundation for Women, a national fund that supports grassroots projects to empower women and girls.

Steinem was a founder of Take Our Daughters to Work Day, the first national day devoted to encouraging young women to think about diverse career options, which has become an institution in many countries worldwide.

Her books include the bestsellers *My Life on the Road*, *Revolution from Within*, *Outrageous Acts and Everyday Rebellions*, *Moving Beyond Words*, *Marilyn: Norma Jean* and *As If Women Matter*. In 2013, President Obama awarded her the Presidential Medal of Freedom, the highest civilian honour in the United States.

While she has undoubtedly brought greater attention and prominence to the movement, her career-long commitment to sharing her platform with other activists means that one of Steinem's greatest influences on the movement itself has been to highlight the importance of cooperation, intersectionality and grassroots organizing. As she herself has put it: 'When unique voices are united in a common cause, they make history.'

Laura Bates

EVERYDAY SEXISM

30-second feminism

In 2012, a series of publicized
escalating experiences of sexism, sexual
harassment and assault led to a re-examination
of the normalization of gender inequality in
daily life, initially in the UK but with stories
soon being added from different countries
worldwide. Once the dialogue was opened,
the frequency and severity of the stories of
everyday women became clear, and countered
claims that sexism no longer existed and that
'women are equal now'. Cue the Everyday
Sexism Project, a collection of testimonies
of individual women's experiences of sexism,
collected on a single website, to raise awareness
of the scale and reality of the problem. In three
years, over 100,000 stories were shared with the
project, creating an international conversation,
from *The New York Times* to *The Times of India*
and sparking a worldwide movement. The
project spread to encompass over 20 branches
in different countries, and its entries started
to be used to create change, campaigning
for better sex and relationships education,
retraining police officers on how to tackle sexual
offences, and even compelling Facebook to
change its policies on rape and sexual violence
content. The phrase 'everyday sexism' has
since become popularized, regularly appearing
outside the context of the project itself.

3-SECOND SLAM
Founded in 2012, the
Everyday Sexism Project
is a website and global
movement that records
and fights against daily
experiences of gender
inequality.

3-MINUTE SPEECH
The term 'everyday sexism'
was intended to convey
multiple meanings. First,
it sought to prove that
these occurrences are a
daily reality for women.
Second, it captures
the normalization and
acceptability of sexism
within society. Third,
the project and phrase
highlight the continuum
whereby the minor
injustices we ignore and
excuse are related to more
serious crimes of gendered
violence and assault, as
part of a wider pattern of
systemic inequality.

RELATED TEXTS
See also
THE RISE OF ONLINE
FEMINISM
page 32

CONSCIOUSNESS-RAISING
page 62

#FEMINISM
page 152

3-SECOND BIOGRAPHY
LAURA BATES
1986–
British writer and feminist
activist, founder of the
Everyday Sexism Project.

30-SECOND TEXT
Laura Bates

*The Everyday Sexism
Project has highlighted
the pervasiveness of
inequality women still
face in daily life.*

INTERSECTIONALITY

30-second feminism

3-SECOND SLAM
Intersectionality refers
to the ways in which
different forms of
inequality may intersect,
so that those who face
more than one type of
oppression experience
a cumulative impact.

3-MINUTE SPEECH
Black feminist writers and
campaigners have stressed
the importance of tackling
multiple forms of prejudice,
explaining that feminist
activism will only ultimately
be effective if it is inclusive
of and beneficial to
all women, not just a
privileged few. In her book
Feminism is for Everybody,
author and activist bell
hooks wrote: 'As long as
women are using class or
race power to dominate
other women, feminist
sisterhood cannot be
fully realized.'

The term 'intersectionality' was coined by American scholar and civil rights advocate Kimberlé Crenshaw in 1989 as a means of explaining the multiple and intersecting forms of oppression faced by black women, which cannot be fully explained either as racism or sexism, but rather as an amalgamation of the two. Crenshaw gave the example of a case in which black female workers claimed they'd been discriminated against on the grounds of race and sex by General Motors, which had hired no black women prior to 1964 and sacked all black women hired after 1970 in mass layoffs. Yet the court wouldn't allow the plaintiffs to create 'a new classification of black women', and argued it could not have been sex discrimination because white women had been hired. The court subsequently dismissed the race discrimination complaint. Intersectionality has since been adapted to apply to other multiple types of oppression (for example, on the grounds of sexuality, gender identity, disability, age, class, caste or religion) and the concept has become one of the most important frameworks for modern feminism. Intersectionality is evident both statistically and in women's testimonies of their own lived experience. In the US, for example, black women working full time make 63 cents to each dollar earned by a white man, compared to 79 cents for white women.

RELATED TEXTS
See also
WOMANISM
page 20

BLACK FEMINISM
page 126

QUEERING FEMINISM
page 130

3-SECOND BIOGRAPHIES
AUDRE LORDE
1934–92
Poet and womanist who
explored racism, sexism
and homophobia.

PATRICIA HILL COLLINS
1948–
Professor whose book *Black
Feminist Thought* explores
oppression experienced by
African-American women

KIMBERLÉ CRENSHAW
1959–
American civil rights advocate
and law professor who coined
the term intersectionality.

30-SECOND TEXT
Laura Bates

*Intersectionality's scope
has widened to refer to
how any forms of
oppression can combine.*

FEMINIST ECONOMICS

30-second feminism

3-SECOND SLAM
Feminist economics uses a feminist lens to examine and critique economic theory, policy and inquiry, and create new economic theory from a gendered, feminist perspective.

3-MINUTE SPEECH
Feminist macroeconomic theories try to influence theoretical models of our economies, by demonstrating the gendered aspects of issues such as fiscal austerity, monetary policy and international trade. This often involves a technique called 'gender disaggregation', where macroeconomic variables are studied by gender, to reveal, for example, how the feminization of labour stimulates investment. So we learn that countries are more likely to recover from economic downturns if women are encouraged into the labour market.

For generations, economists created models of our society and economy focussed exclusively on male-centric concerns such as employment and production, but omitting the unpaid, unrecorded caregiving and homemaking work done by millions of women. As this work was undervalued and unpaid, it was invisible to economists, yet feminists argued that it was only because of women doing this work, day in, day out, that men were free to perform paid jobs and make money. Feminist economics pioneered alternative models, taking a broader, gendered perspective of social and economic contexts. In 1988, Marilyn Waring published the book *If Women Counted*, the 'founding document' of feminist economics, warning: 'Men won't easily give up a system in which half the world's population works for next to nothing.' Feminist economists highlight 'unofficial' revenue streams from activities such as illegal arms, drugs and human trafficking, which disproportionately enrich men. They've demonstrated the ways in which economic upheaval and shift – resulting from industrialization, globalization and other structural changes – have different impacts on men and women. The result has been a push for more varied methodologies and approaches to include a broader range of people's experiences.

RELATED TEXTS
See also
FEMINISM IN INSTITUTIONS
page 24

MATERNITY LEAVE & CHILDCARE
page 106

3-SECOND BIOGRAPHIES
ESTER BOSERUP
1910–99
Danish and French economist who advanced the view that women's role in economic development was undervalued.

BINA AGARWAL
1951–
Prize-winning development economist whose work has had a significant international impact in promoting women's rights to land and property.

MARILYN WARING
1952–
New Zealand academic, feminist, politician and founder of feminist economics.

30-SECOND TEXT
Laura Bates

Feminist economics takes into account the 'invisible' labour of women.

AGAINST PATRIARCHY

AGAINST PATRIARCHY
GLOSSARY

capitalism Economic system based on private ownership of industry and trade for profit.

domestic violence Includes physical, emotional and sexual abuse in couple relationships or between family members or by carers.

gay liberation movement Sought to end discrimination against gays, lesbians, bisexuals and transsexuals; embraced aggressive tactics throughout the 1970s, when the movement became prolific.

hegemonic masculinity Describes how men and boys must perform particular cultural practices in order to access the privileges of male power.

homophobia Dislike or prejudice against people who are lesbian, gay or bisexual.

incel (involuntarily celibate) Online community dominated by men who believe they have been denied their right of sexual access to women.

intersectionality The multiple and intersecting forms of oppression faced by black women and others.

kyriarchy From the Greek kyrios (master); a system in which women are not simply oppressed by men under the social structure of patriarchy, but live under multiple systems of oppression that interact with one another.

lads' mags Men's lifestyle magazines that often feature scantily dressed women, epitomizing the laddish culture of the 1990s and 2000s.

men's rights activists (MRAs) Explicitly anti-feminist male movement.

#MeToo Online campaign run by Tarana Burke since 2005, used to share experiences of sexual harassment and violence.

molest Sexually assault or abuse, especially a woman or child.

patriarchy The systematic dominance of men over women. Men hold the power and dominate in roles of political leadership, moral authority, social privilege and control of property.

pornography (porn) Any media that portrays sexually explicit material for the purpose of sexual arousal. Many feminists argue that all pornography is demeaning to women and even provokes violence towards women.

Power and Control Wheel tool (Also called the Duluth Model) Used by social workers to explain how abusive partners use not only physical and sexual abuse, but also emotional, psychological and financial abuse to control their partners.

prostitution Engaging in sexual activity in exchange for payment. Legality varies the world over, and while some feminists argue against all forms of prostitution as being degrading to women and exploiting male dominance, others argue that unforced sex work can be a valid choice.

racism Belief that one race or ethnicity is superior over another. Patricia Bidol contended that racism occurs when prejudice is combined with institutional power.

sexism Prejudice or discrimination based on sex or gender, especially against women and girls.

SlutWalk Global movement campaigning for an end to rape culture and, in particular, blaming the victim for the assault.

toxic masculinity Stereotypically masculine gender roles that limit the scope of male emotions due to social expectations and make patriarchy harmful to men.

white supremacy Racist belief in the superiority of white people over other races, which is rooted in scientific racism and has been used as a political ideology in the regimes of Nazi Germany and Apartheid South Africa, and to justify slavery in the US. This term is often used to describe pervasive, institutional racism as a defining structure of society.

women's refuge/shelter Safe-house where women and children who are experiencing domestic abuse can stay, free from fear.

PATRIARCHY

30-second feminism

In patriarchal societies, men are the heads of households, dominate positions of leadership outside the home and control most of the society's resources. In both the UK and the US in the 1970s, feminists seized on the idea that they were living in a 'patriarchy', to explain women's continuing inequality. Building on arguments in Kate Millett's *Sexual Politics*, published in 1970, feminists argued that men's oppression of women in intimate relationships was the foundation of women's inequality in society more broadly. Importantly, feminists contended that men upheld their power by controlling financial resources in the family and using violence against their wives, girlfriends and daughters. The activism that followed focused on disrupting men's power over women in relationships: supporting women to leave violent partners, fighting for contraception and abortion, and securing family legal rights like divorce, child custody and child support. Resistance to patriarchy in the 1970s achieved enduring wins for women's rights, including the establishment of a national federation of domestic violence refuges in many countries and the right to abortion on demand in the US, with the Supreme Court's judgement in Roe v. Wade. The concept of patriarchy remains central to much contemporary feminist activism, such as the #MeToo movement against sexual violence.

3-SECOND SLAM
Feminists in the 1970s campaigned against a society dominated by men – 'the patriarchy' – to campaign for women's rights in work, the family and over their own bodies.

3-MINUTE SPEECH
Ever since *Sexual Politics* brought patriarchy to the mainstream, feminists have recognized the limits of its ability to fully explain gender inequality. The black feminist author bell hooks, who was also active in the 1970s movement, has interrogated how patriarchy interacts with other systems of power such as capitalism and white supremacy, and the negative impact patriarchy has on men and boys.

RELATED TEXTS
See also
WOMEN'S LIBERATION MOVEMENT
page 18

CHOICE & ABORTION
page 100

#FEMINISM
page 152

3-SECOND BIOGRAPHIES
KATE MILLETT
1934–2017
American feminist whose book *Sexual Politics* popularized the theory of patriarchy.

BELL HOOKS
1952–
American author whose book *Ain't I A Woman?* critiqued the exclusion of black women in the feminist movement.

30-SECOND TEXT
Shannon Harvey

Radical feminists view patriarchy as the main cause of women's oppression.

REFUGE MOVEMENT
30-second feminism

3-SECOND SLAM
Feminist volunteers opened the first refuges in the 1970s, allowing women who had few legal rights to leave their violent husbands.

3-MINUTE SPEECH
Chiswick Women's Aid went on to become the UK charity Refuge, but its founder Erin Pizzey never considered herself a feminist. Eventually, Pizzey became a men's rights activist, arguing that the women she supported had frequently admitted to using violence themselves. With the professionalization of the refuge movement, the response to domestic violence has become less explicitly feminist, often being led through local government, the police or through mainstream housing charities.

In a crumbling, overcrowded building in West London in 1971, Chiswick Women's Aid became the first refuge for women fleeing domestic violence. Public and open to the media, the women's stories of their husbands' violence shone a light on the brutal reality of domestic violence. Feminist activists quickly saw the potential of refuges as a way to liberate abused women who still had few rights in family law. Volunteer-run refuges for women fleeing domestic violence began to open around the UK, and the idea spread through the 1970s' women's liberation movement, with women's shelters opening across Europe, in the US and in Australia. These volunteer-run refuges gradually evolved into formal charities with professional staff and specialist refuges opened for black and minority ethnic women, and later for women with mental health, drug and alcohol issues. Through their experience of running refuges, feminists also expanded public understandings of domestic violence. In Duluth, Minnesota, feminists developed the influential 'Power and Control Wheel' tool to explain how abusive partners use not only physical and sexual abuse, but emotional, psychological and financial abuse to retain control over their partners.

RELATED TEXTS
See also
WOMEN'S LIBERATION MOVEMENT
page 18

FEMINISM IN INSTITUTIONS
page 24

FAMILY LAW REFORM
page 86

3-SECOND BIOGRAPHY
ERIN PIZZEY
1939–
Opened Chiswick Women's Aid in 1971, the first refuge for women fleeing domestic violence.

30-SECOND TEXT
Shannon Harvey

Erin Pizzey focused on breaking the cycle of domestic abuse by removing victims from their abusers.

26 September 1946
Born in Camden,
New Jersey

1955
Molested at nine
years old

1965
Testifies to being
assaulted by doctors
in detention, following
her arrest at an anti-war
protest

1968
Graduates with a degree
in literature from
Bennington, a women's
college in Vermont

1969
Moves to Amsterdam and
marries Cornelius Dirk
de Bruin, who severely
abuses her

1971
Flees her abusive
marriage, becoming
homeless in the
Netherlands and selling
sex to survive

1972
Meets Ricki Abrams,
who introduces her
to American radical
feminist writings

1972
Begins writing *Woman
Hating* with Ricki Abrams,
and returns to the US

1974
Meets gay feminist
activist John Stoltenberg,
who becomes her life
partner until her death

1974
Publishes her first book,
*Woman Hating: A Radical
Look at Sexuality*

1976
Helps organize public
pickets of the splatter
horror film *Snuff* in New
York City

1978
Addresses the first Take
Back The Night march in
San Francisco

1981
Publishes *Pornography:
Men Possessing Women*

1983
With Catharine
MacKinnon, drafts an
antipornography civil
rights ordinance for
Minneapolis

1986
Testifies against the
pornography industry
to the Meese Commission
in New York City

1989
Publishes *Intercourse*,
extending her arguments
against pornography to
heterosexual intercourse

2002
Publishes autobiography,
*Heartbreak: The Political
Memoir of a Feminist
Militant*

9 April 2005
Dies at age 58 at her
home in Washington, DC

ANDREA DWORKIN

Rooted in her own experiences of abuse, Andrea Dworkin's uncompromising writings against male violence galvanized feminist activism against pornography and prostitution. Over her life, she developed her analysis of how men's performance of sexual domination through pornography facilitated other forms of violence against women.

Dworkin's activism was deeply informed by multiple, horrific experiences of violence during her childhood and young adulthood. At nine years old, she was molested in her home town. Ten years later, following her arrest at an anti-Vietnam war demonstration, she was sexually assaulted by doctors while in detention. In her early 20s, her first husband, Dutch anarchist Cornelius Dirk de Bruin, brutally beat her and burned her with cigarettes. When she fled his abuse, she became homeless and was forced into prostitution to survive.

At this lowest point, stranded in the Netherlands, Dworkin met Ricki Abrams. Abrams introduced her to American radical feminist writings and together, they began writing her first book. Finished after she returned to the United States, *Woman Hating* describes how violent cultural practices are used to subjugate women globally, from Chinese foot-binding to pornography. Over the next seven years, Dworkin developed her thinking around male violence, and in *Pornography*, argues that prostitution and pornography are inherently exploitative, a means through which men possess women. Later, in *Intercourse*, she extended this argument to posit that heterosexual sex itself is a site of potential subordination of women.

Dworkin's writings were often based on her speeches, given at rallies and marches around the United States. She spoke passionately and eloquently about men's violence against women. Her activism went beyond protest, however. In the early 1980s, Dworkin worked with feminist legal scholar Catharine MacKinnon to frame pornography as a women's civil rights issue. Hired by the city of Minneapolis, they drafted a civil rights ordinance which defined pornography as a civil rights violation, which, if passed, would have allowed women to sue producers and distributors for harm caused.

Despite her untimely death from acute myocarditis at the age of 58, Dworkin's influence continues in radical feminist campaigns today. In the UK, her arguments are present in campaigns against 'lads' mags', and in support of the criminalization of men who pay for sex. However, in feminist movements more broadly, her arguments have largely been overtaken by intersectional analyses that prioritize sex workers' autonomy and rights.

Shannon Harvey

FAMILY LAW REFORM

30-second feminism

3-SECOND SLAM
Recognizing that laws around the family protected men's position of power, feminists sought reforms to increase women and children's rights within and after marriage.

3-MINUTE SPEECH
Apparently progressive developments in family law over the past decades have sometimes had unforeseen negative consequences for women. In Australia, a family law presumption of equal co-parenting after divorce has been used by abusers to manipulate their former partners, while in the UK, recognition of domestic abuse as a form of child abuse has resulted in women having their children removed from them if they don't leave a violent partner.

Through opening refuges for women fleeing domestic abuse, activists were forced to confront the way laws related to family relationships discriminated against women. Women who left abusive husbands often found themselves destitute and fighting to retain custody of their children. Feminists responded with broad-ranging campaigns to reform family law. Child 'maintenance' or 'support' laws were won in jurisdictions around the world between the 1970s and 1990s, following campaigns for fathers to contribute financially to their children's upbringing, even if they were not living with them. Feminists also highlighted the ongoing risks women faced after fleeing their abusive partner, when they were required to facilitate access to children. Improved measures were gradually introduced, including supervised custody visits and measures to prevent the abuser contacting their former partner, such as domestic violence restraining orders in the UK and civil protection orders in the US. Alongside campaigns for rights on leaving a marriage, women fought to reform laws within the institution of marriage. In the UK, landmark cases such as that of Kiranjit Ahluwalia in 1989 recognized domestic violence victimization as a defence to murder, and R v R in 1991 recognized the possibility of rape within marriage.

RELATED TEXTS
See also
FEMINISM IN INSTITUTIONS
page 24

REFUGE MOVEMENT
page 82

RAPE CULTURE
page 88

3-SECOND BIOGRAPHY
KIRANJIT AHLUWALIA
1955–
Killed her husband following a decade of domestic abuse, and was later supported by London-based Asian women's organization Southall Black Sisters to appeal her murder conviction.

30-SECOND TEXT
Shannon Harvey

Laws governing marriage, divorce, child custody and property ownership have all been critiqued by feminists.

RAPE CULTURE

30-second feminism

RELATED TEXTS
See also
CONSCIOUSNESS-RAISING
page 62

#FEMINISM
page 152

3-SECOND BIOGRAPHIES
SUSAN BROWNMILLER
1935–
Journalist who published the bestselling *Against Our Will*, cataloguing the ways rape had been used throughout history to control women.

TARANA BURKE
1973–
Activist who founded the MeToo campaign on MySpace in 2006, which went viral in 2017 as #MeToo, following rape allegations against Hollywood producer Harvey Weinstein.

30-SECOND TEXT
Shannon Harvey

3-SECOND SLAM
Through telling their personal stories of sexual assault, feminists have shown the cultural pervasiveness of rape as a tool of male power.

3-MINUTE SPEECH
Activism against rape culture has become increasingly globalized in the digital age. Worldwide SlutWalk marches followed a Canadian police officer's suggestion in 2011 that women avoid rape by not dressing 'like sluts', and global protests followed the brutal gang rape of Jyoti Singh in Delhi in 2012. In 2017, women and men joined global Women's Marches in record numbers following the inauguration of US President Donald Trump, who was heard boasting about sexually assaulting women.

An important feature of feminist activism in the 1970s was the promotion of women's stories of their experiences of sexism. As women began sharing their personal accounts of sexual assault, they demonstrated that rape was not just a personal trauma, but it was also a pervasive social problem. Feminists began to call out a society that encouraged and defended men's systematic use of rape to maintain control over women: a rape culture. Feminists analysed the cultural beliefs and practices that promoted the idea that women's bodies are men's sexual property, from advertising, through dress, to legislation. Further, black feminists examined how colonialism systematically sexualized women of colour, creating a culture in which they continue to experience rape disproportionately. In 1972, the first rape crisis centre was established in Washington, DC, providing support for survivors and lobbying for legislative change. Feminists won important battles over the following decades, such as the criminalization of rape in marriage in the US and UK in the 1990s. Services expanded, with more rape crisis centres, specialist roles within the police, training for judges and publicly funded awareness-raising campaigns.

Through sharing accounts of personal trauma, women realized that rape was a systemic control tactic.

THE POLITICS OF MASCULINITY

30-second feminism

As the women's liberation movement was rising in the 1970s, so was the gay liberation movement. While always closely connected, by the 1990s, gay men and trans women's critiques of cultural norms around masculinity began to be more clearly integrated into feminist arguments and campaigning. Australian academic Raewyn Connell first used the term 'hegemonic masculinity' in the early 1980s to describe how men and boys must perform particular cultural practices in order to access the privileges of male power. For example, in Western cultures, boys may be expected not to cry, and be berated for acting 'like a girl' if they do. As feminists explored the ways they were harmed by social constructions of what it means to be a woman, gay and trans activists explored the same concerns around constructions of what it means to be a man. Gay and women's rights activists began to argue together for a more diverse understanding of femininity and masculinity. In fact, taking it a step further, Canadian queer philosopher Judith Butler argued women's experiences of womanhood were so different depending on how they were impacted by class and race, for example, that we must talk of genders, femininities and masculinities.

3-SECOND SLAM
From the 1980s, activists began to describe how men were also oppressed by patriarchy, by being expected to perform their masculinity.

3-MINUTE SPEECH
Connell's ideas are evident today in the more commonly used term 'toxic masculinity'. Despite positive shifts in cultural practices associated with male power (for example, men doing a greater share of unpaid housework), there has also been a backlash. The online incel (involuntarily celibate) community is dominated by men who believe they have been denied their right of sexual access to women, and the movement has been associated with fatal mass shootings in the US.

RELATED TEXTS
See also
BACKLASH
page 36

QUEERING FEMINISM
page 130

WHIPPING GIRL
page 132

3-SECOND BIOGRAPHY
RAEWYN CONNELL
1944–
Australian sociologist and trans woman whose 1995 book, *Masculinities*, set out her theory of hegemonic masculinity.

30-SECOND TEXT
Shannon Harvey

Gender stereotyping has proved to be harmful for men as well as women.

FROM PATRIARCHY TO KYRIARCHY

30-second feminism

RELATED TEXTS
See also
INTERSECTIONALITY
page 72

BLACK FEMINISM
page 126

3-SECOND SLAM
Realizing the limits of the concept of patriarchy, some feminists looked to a new idea – kyriarchy – to explain how different power structures interact.

3-MINUTE SPEECH
In a patriarchy, all women are oppressed and all men are oppressors. However, in a kyriarchy, everyone is both oppressor and oppressed, depending on their position in a particular context. As black activist Angela Davis argued in the early 1980s, even in the feminist movement itself, white women asserted their power over black women to prioritize their own, narrow fights for equality.

While 1970s feminist campaigning was coalescing around the concept of patriarchy, black feminists were simultaneously arguing patriarchy's limitations. Writers such as bell hooks described how white women used the structures of slavery and racism to maintain power over black men, and how black women were oppressed by both sexism and racism. As these discussions developed, it became clear that patriarchy was insufficient to explain the ways that all women were discriminated against as women. At the end of the 1980s, the now-ubiquitous term 'intersectionality' was coined to describe how black women experienced sexism in specific, racialized ways. Building on this, feminist theologian Elisabeth Schüssler Fiorenza proposed the term 'kyriarchy' – drawing on the Greek word *kyrios* (master) – as an alternative to patriarchy. In Schüssler Fiorenza's kyriarchy, women are not simply oppressed by men under the social structure of patriarchy, but live under multiple systems of oppression that interact with one another: sexism, racism, homophobia, economic injustice and more. With an explosion of feminist blogging in the late 2000s, a post by one of Schüssler Fiorenza's students, Lisa Factora-Borchers, helped popularize the concept. The term was embraced as a way to acknowledge and discuss social structures of power beyond the limitations of patriarchy.

3-SECOND BIOGRAPHIES
ELISABETH SCHÜSSLER FIORENZA
1938–
Feminist theologian and author of *But She Said: Feminist Practices of Biblical Interpretation*.

ANGELA DAVIS
1944–
Published *Women, Race and Class*, describing how the women's liberation movement in the US represented white middle-class women.

KIMBERLÉ CRENSHAW
1959–
Coined 'intersectionality' to describe how systems of oppression intersect.

30-SECOND TEXT
Shannon Harvey

Kyriarchy recognizes that women are oppressed by more than the patriarchy.

MY BODY, MY CHOICE

MY BODY, MY CHOICE
GLOSSARY

abortion The act of deliberately ending a pregnancy by removing an embryo or foetus; legality and cultural beliefs differ widely across the globe and within countries or even regions.

bodily autonomy The right to self governance over one's own body, without external influence or coercion.

contraception Ways of preventing pregnancy that became readily available in the twentieth century, although are still stigmatized and/or outlawed in some cultures and countries. The widespread access to and use of contraceptive methods has been linked to the sexual liberation of women.

First Nations Predominant indigenous peoples in Canada, south of the Arctic Circle, who are not Métis or Inuit.

forcible sterilization Ending someone's ability to reproduce without his or her consent. Applied through government policy and largely to women from minority groups.

gendered Describes how an experience is affected by the gender of the subject, or how something particularly affects people differently based on their gender.

heteronormativity The belief that people fall into distinct and complementary genders (male and female) with natural roles in life, including heterosexuality as the normal or preferred sexual orientation and cisgender as the default identification.

heterosexism Discrimination against LGBTQI people and assumption that opposite-sex relationships and sexuality are the norm.

institutionalized culture Exists when certain conceptions (a belief, norm, social role, value or behaviour) are embedded within a social system, or society as a whole.

LGBTQI Umbrella term for the lesbian, gay, bisexual, transgender, questioning/queer, and intersex community.

prenatal testing Consists of screening and diagnostic processes designed to detect problems or defects with the pregnancy and/or embryo. Ethically questionable, such practices have been associated with upholding disability stereotyping and leading to selective abortion.

pro-choice Those who support the right to abortion. The term emerged from North American campaigning groups in the 1960s. 'Pro-life' campaigners are opposed to abortion.

reproductive justice Term coined by the SisterSong Reproductive Health Collective in the 1990s, who stated that it is 'the human right to maintain personal bodily autonomy, have children, not have children, and parent the children we have in safe and sustainable communities.'

selective abortion Deciding to terminate a pregnancy when the foetus is perceived as having undesirable characteristics.

sex-positive feminism Began in the early 1980s and focused on sexual freedom as an essential component of women's freedom.

sexual consent Agreement, without threat, coercion or force, to engage in a sexual act. There can be many factors that constitute legal consent, which play an important role in defining sexual assault.

social justice Fairness and equality in the distribution of wealth, opportunities and privileges within a society.

social model of disability Reaction to the medical model of disability which reflects the complex interaction between features of a person's body with the features of the society in which they live, meaning that society can be the main factor in disabling people.

social mores Customs, norms, behaviours and practices that are acceptable to a society or social group.

women of colour (WOC) Political term used to collectively describe females of colour; emerged in the violence against women movement and became a unifying term in the 1970s for all minority women experiencing marginalization, with race and ethnicity as a common factor.

WOMEN & SEXUAL LIBERATION

30-second feminism

RELATED TEXTS
See also
OBJECTIFICATION
page 64

BODY POSITIVITY
page 66

RAPE CULTURE
page 88

3-SECOND SLAM
Male-dominant science, culture and politics continue to promote the sexual-political control of women by men, as they have done throughout the ages.

3-MINUTE SPEECH
Throughout the history of patriarchy, in all parts of the world, women's sexuality has been a site of oppression, if in different ways. Sometimes, women's sexual behaviour led to diagnoses of hysteria; sometimes it led to the surgical removal of parts of their genitals; sometimes women were told that they 'owed' sex to their husbands. Women's oppression is often conflated with desire, perhaps most obviously in mainstream pornography, advertising, music videos and game consoles.

For the most part, both sexual repression and sexual liberation have been associated with women's oppression. Historically, women who expressed their sexuality suffered repercussions, especially when they did so outside of heterosexual marriage. In 1921, a scientist named Margaret Sanger founded the American Birth Control League and began developing a pharmaceutical birth-control product. In 1960, when the oral contraceptive pill was approved for use, there was, for the first time, a way to separate sexual intercourse and reproduction, which led to new patterns of sexual behaviour among heterosexual women and men. The pill was followed by the second-wave feminist movement, which focused, among others, on female sexual pleasure and vaginal orgasm. Subsequently, it was banned in many parts of the world. Even in the West, it was so scandalous that a song (Lorretta Lynn's 'The Pill') about the freedoms the pill gave women was banned. Feminist activism and theory has since advanced on the second wave by addressing issues such as consent and the destigmatization of female masturbation as well as the emergence of sex-positive feminism. With the stories of harassment and violence shared online today, it is clear that sexual liberation has hardly even begun.

3-SECOND BIOGRAPHY
MARGARET SANGER
1879–1966
Birth control activist, women's rights campaigner, writer and nurse who coined the term 'birth control' and opened the first birth control centre in the US.

30-SECOND TEXT
Minna Salami

Availability of and access to birth control were just the start of women's sexual liberation.

CHOICE & ABORTION

30-second feminism

The act of deliberately ending a pregnancy – abortion – represents, to feminists, a fundamental right for women, granting as it does the choice of when, how and whether to have children. Without access to safe and legal abortion, women who have unwanted pregnancies face two choices: to continue the pregnancy or to obtain an illegal and potentially unsafe abortion. The feminist fight for legal abortion has sought to prevent forced pregnancies and give women more control over their reproductive lives. Those who support the right to abortion are therefore called 'pro-choice', a term that emerged from North American campaigning groups in the 1960s. Abortion was legalized in many countries in the 1960s and 1970s on the back of pro-choice feminist activism that emerged across the globe. This happened alongside growing acceptance of contraception and family planning in many countries. The United Nations now recognizes access to abortion as a fundamental human right. There are some countries that still heavily restrict or completely ban it, however, including Poland, Malta and El Salvador. These countries tend to be highly religious.

3-SECOND SLAM
Access to abortion offers the choice to continue or end pregnancies; for feminists, this is a fundamental right that allows women to control their bodies and lives.

3-MINUTE SPEECH
While in most countries abortion is *legalized* (i.e. it is now legal under certain circumstances), there are some countries which have completely *decriminalized* abortion (i.e. they have removed all criminal law relating to abortion). One example is Canada, where no legal restrictions on abortion have existed since 1988. Proponents argue that decriminalization is preferable as it removes government regulation of abortion, offers women freer reproductive choice and removes the threat of criminalization from those seeking and providing abortions.

RELATED TEXTS
See also
THE FIGHT FOR RIGHTS IN PREGNANCY & LABOUR
page 102

DISABILITY & ABORTION
page 108

SISTERSONG'S REPRODUCTIVE JUSTICE MANIFESTO
page 112

3-SECOND BIOGRAPHIES
HENRY MORGENTALER
1923–2013
Canadian doctor who gave women abortions in defiance of the law and won a court case which decriminalized abortion in Canada in 1988.

REBECCA GOMPERTS
1966–
Physician who founded Women on Waves, providing services on a ship outside territorial waters for women in countries where abortion is illegal.

30-SECOND TEXT
Gillian Love

No matter the law, women need and find ways to access abortion across the globe.

THE FIGHT FOR RIGHTS IN PREGNANCY & LABOUR

30-second feminism

The fight for pregnancy and

labour rights does not begin and end with the struggle for accessible contraception and legal, safe abortions. Feminists have also fought for adequate woman-centred maternity care that respects the dignity, choices and consent of pregnant women. The history of childbirth has not always focused on the needs of expectant mothers. Much formal medical advice from physicians was formed by guesswork, as social mores kept men out of the delivery room – childbirth was deemed a private, feminine affair. Maternal death rates were high and pain relief was rarely provided: many regarded pain in childbirth as a heavenly duty; a necessary pain women must suffer as a punishment for Eve's sins in the Garden of Eden. This was replaced in much of the world by a time of pregnancy controlled by overwhelmingly male doctors, with midwives excluded and sometimes banned, and practices such as strapping women to the bed during labour being introduced. Thankfully, much has changed. As well as the introduction of handwashing and anaesthetics to the birthing process, which have lowered death rates and unnecessary pain, women's rights advocates have sought to ensure that medical professionals seek consent for any treatments and that this consent be well-informed and freely given by patients.

3-SECOND SLAM
Pregnancy and labour provide fertile ground for the fight for women's bodily rights and autonomy.

3-MINUTE SPEECH
As more and more women have entered the workforce, feminists have also demanded freedom from discrimination at work while pregnant. Until the introduction of various legislative changes, many working women lost their jobs or were placed on unpaid leave merely for becoming pregnant. Tireless campaigns in a number of countries have seen feminists win paid maternity leave and, in some cases, paid paternity leave, so that the responsibilities of child rearing can be shared more easily.

RELATED TEXTS
See also
BODY POSITIVITY
page 66

WOMEN & SEXUAL LIBERATION
page 98

CHOICE & ABORTION
page 100

3-SECOND BIOGRAPHIES
SARA JOSEPHINE BAKER
1873–1945
Pioneering American physician in the field of public health care, particularly women and children, and women's rights activist.

MARGARET SANGER
1879–1966
American birth control activist and sex educator.

SHEILA KITZINGER
1929–2015
British natural childbirth activist and author.

30-SECOND TEXT
Nadia Mehdi

Maternity rights are as crucial for bodily autonomy as access to abortion.

30 April 1977
The first march of the
Mothers of the Plaza
de Mayo

December 1977
Two of the founders of
the Mothers of the Plaza
de Mayo, Esther Careaga
and Eugenia Bianco,
disappear. On the
International Day of
Human Rights, the
mothers publish a
newspaper story with
the names of the missing
children; founder
Azucena Villaflor
disappears, reported to
have been thrown into
the sea from a plane.

1978
FIFA World Cup is held in
Argentina, the mothers'
demonstrations are
covered by the
international press

1982
Association swells from
14 mothers to several
thousand women

1983
Fall of the military
dictatorship; mothers
transform themselves
into a political group,
marching every week
to seek justice for the
disappeared

2005
The remains of
disappeared founder
Azucena Villaflor are
recovered and her ashes
are buried in the Plaza
de Mayo

2016
More than 1,000 of the
dictatorship's murderers
and torturers have been
tried, with 700 sentenced

2018
128 babies born to
disappeared mothers
and illegally adopted
by military families
are reunited with their
biological families
as adults

THE MOTHERS OF THE PLAZA DE MAYO

The Mothers of the Plaza de

Mayo is an association of Argentinian women whose children were disappeared during the military dictatorship of 1976–1983. On 30th April 1977, 14 mothers – who had met in the waiting room of a government building while searching for information about their missing children – decided to demonstrate in the Plaza de Mayo, Buenos Aires, the location of the presidential building, La Casa Rosada. This direct action was in defiance of the state's attempt to silence all opposition.

The mothers wore white headscarves, embroidered with the names of their disappeared children, to symbolize the nappies of their lost children and a refusal to go in to mourning. Since public gathering in groups of more than three or four was not allowed, they would march around the square in pairs to avoid arrest. They have continued their demonstrations weekly for the past four decades.

The Mothers declare that during the decade between 1970 and 1980, more than 30,000 people were erased from public records, with no traces of arrest. Most are presumed dead, but around 500 are thought to be people born to pregnant disappeared women who were murdered after giving birth, with the babies being illegally adopted by military families to avoid raising another generation of subversives.

Three of the founders of the Mothers of the Plaza de Mayo – Azucena Villaflor, Esther Careaga and Eugenia Bianco – were themselves kidnapped, tortured, murdered and disappeared by the government.

The Mothers of the Plaza de Mayo were the first large group to organize against the human rights violations committed by the military dictatorship, and it is a strictly women-only organization. The idea behind this was threefold: they didn't want their voices and actions to be lost in a male-dominated movement; they believed that men might insist on lengthy bureaucratic and legislative procedures to recover their children over immediate action; and they believed women to be more tireless and have more emotional strength than men. The government initially tried to trivialize their efforts, calling them *'las locas'*, the mad women, yet their perseverance brought them both local and international coverage and acclaim.

Since the war the mothers have continued organizing tirelessly for justice for their disappeared family members and to reunite any surviving disappeared people with their biological families. They will continue to refuse bribes and governmental declarations of 'presumed dead' as long as those officials involved in the disappearances go free.

Nadia Mehdi

MATERNITY LEAVE & CHILDCARE

30-second feminism

3-SECOND SLAM
The problem: motherhood is correlated with lower participation in the workforce and diminished salaries; a solution: paid parental leave, universal childcare and domestic workers' rights.

3-MINUTE SPEECH
In the United States, childcare workers are among the most undercompensated employees in any occupation. Persistent advocacy by the National Domestic Workers Alliance on behalf of childcare and other domestic workers resulted in New York State passing the nation's first 'Domestic Workers' Bill of Rights' in 2010. This legislation provides protections such as paid leave and overtime pay to the low-income women of colour, who are the majority of the state's childcare workers.

Maternity leave – paid and unpaid – became increasingly prevalent throughout the twentieth century, enabling women to return to their jobs after becoming parents. In response to feminist lobbying, Mexico's 1917 constitution provided a month of paid maternity leave. By the early 1950s, countries like South Korea and Japan gave women 60 to 90 days of paid leave. Except for Swaziland, Lesotho, Papua New Guinea and the United States, most countries now offer new mothers at least three months of paid leave, and many offer time off to parents, regardless of gender. Paid parental (rather than maternity) leave sends a strong message to new fathers and LGBTQI parents that their caregiving roles are equally important. This helps dismantle pre-existing caregiving hierarchies that are strongly structured by gender and legal partnership. Historically, caregiving has usually been women's work, and is undervalued as such. Inadequate or expensive childcare has often led women to reduce their working hours, consolidating a gendered pay gap. As a remedy, some feminists have called for free, universal childcare – a platform of the 1970 Women's Strike for Equality in the US and the current Women's Equality Party in the UK. Others have sought state subsidies or compensation for childcare as unwaged domestic work.

RELATED TEXTS
See also
FAMILY LAW REFORM
page 86

THE FIGHT FOR RIGHTS IN PREGNANCY & LABOUR
page 102

3-SECOND BIOGRAPHIES
BENAZIR BHUTTO & JACINDA ARDERN
1953–2007 & 1980–
Benazir Bhutto, former Prime Minister of Pakistan, was the first elected woman leader to have a child in office (1990); New Zealand Prime Minister Jacinda Ardern was the second, and the first to take maternity leave (2018).

AI-JEN POO
1974–
Executive Director of the National Domestic Workers Alliance; lead organizer of New York's Domestic Workers' Bill of Rights campaign.

30-SECOND TEXT
Sarah Tobias

Parental leave is an inclusive term that enables parents of all genders to take time off work for childcare.

DISABILITY & ABORTION

30-second feminism

3-SECOND SLAM
Prenatal testing and selective abortion are becoming increasingly routinized, but disability rights activists worry about what this says about our attitudes to disability.

3-MINUTE SPEECH
While using prenatal tests has its issues, it is also difficult to delineate acceptable and unacceptable tests. It seems ethically acceptable to test for conditions leading to short lives of intense suffering, but unacceptable to test for vanity traits such as eye colour. Yet deciding which other conditions warrant prenatal testing may involve stigmatizing those with 'serious' conditions and belittling challenges faced by those with 'unserious' conditions.

Feminist disability rights activists have raised compelling concerns over the use of prenatal tests for a variety of genetic and other anomalies. The tests centre on a perceived entrenchment of the Medical Model of Disability, which understands disabilities to be impairments of an individual body, leaving the disabled person unable to perform various functions that an able-bodied person can. In this model, it is the job of medicine to intervene, fixing bodies or mitigating the undesirable effects of disability where it can. The Social Model of Disability, however, takes the view that disabilities are socially constructed. Bodily impairments are simply neutral; disability arises from a lack of accommodations in our current reality. For instance, in a society without a written language, dyslexia is not disabling. Disabilities are understood to be historically specific and context-dependent. Institutionalizing prenatal testing further entrenches the idea that disability is a medical condition detected at the level of individual bodies, rather than a neutral difference that makes life more difficult for people due to inaccessible material environments. Moreover, insofar as abortion is a standard response to such testing, the practice of 'fixing' disability through medical intervention becomes entrenched.

RELATED TEXTS
See also
INTERSECTIONALITY
page 72

CHOICE & ABORTION
page 100

3-SECOND BIOGRAPHY
ROSEMARIE GARLAND THOMSON
fl. 2000–
Disability justice leader, bioethicist, teacher and scholar attributed with establishing the field of feminist disability studies.

30-SECOND TEXT
Nadia Mehdi

Activists urge us to reject the assumption that prenatal testing and abortion are the solutions to disability.

HETEROSEXISM

30-second feminism

Everywhere we look we see depictions of heterosexual relationships as the norm – in films, advertisements, novels, songs, social settings and our families. Moreover, depictions of sexual desire are most often shown as a person of one sex being attracted to a person of the other sex. The nuclear family, monogamy, heterosexual marriage and parenting are socially, culturally and legally sanctioned as the natural way of life. This institutionalized culture – that legitimizes and privileges heterosexual relationships and traditional gender roles – is known as heteronormativity. Heterosexism is the outcome of heteronormativity. It is when a person thinks of heterosexuality as the norm and views other forms of sexuality as inferior, abnormal or less valid. Feminism has been particularly concerned with dismantling heterosexism, which tends to conceive of LGBTQI people as transgressing rigid gender roles. Policing those gender roles is also argued to be integral to the functioning of sexism and patriarchy. For this reason, feminists will sometimes talk about 'heteropatriarchy'. Despite homophobia and heterosexism existing within feminism, many feminists would now argue that it would be impossible to eliminate sexism without also ending heterosexism.

3-SECOND SLAM
Heterosexism was a term coined in the 1970s to explicitly compare discrimination against gay and lesbian people with sexism, racism and other forms of oppression.

3-MINUTE SPEECH
Heterosexuality has not always been seen as the normal mode of romantic intimacy. Relationships between men were socially acceptable and common in Ancient Greece, for example. Similarly, in parts of historical Africa it was not uncommon for women to marry and cohabit a 'female husband', as Nigerian scholar Ifi Amadiume calls it. However, whether these marriages were of a romantic nature is disputed.

RELATED TEXTS
See also
EVERYDAY SEXISM
page 70

PATRIARCHY
page 80

QUEERING FEMINISM
page 130

3-SECOND BIOGRAPHIES
CRAIG RODWELL
1940–93
American gay rights activist who founded the first gay/lesbian-author bookshop and the NYC pride demonstration, and is also thought to have coined the term heterosexism.

IFI AMADIUME
1947–
Nigerian poet, anthropologist, essayist and author of *Male Daughters, Female Husbands*.

30-SECOND TEXT
Minna Salami

Traditional gender roles and family models are being challenged by more unconventional and fluid ways of living.

SISTERSONG'S REPRODUCTIVE JUSTICE MANIFESTO

30-second feminism

RELATED TEXTS
See also
CHOICE & ABORTION
page 100

THE FIGHT FOR RIGHTS IN
PREGNANCY & LABOUR
page 102

DISABILITY & ABORTION
page 108

3-SECOND SLAM
Reproductive justice, coined by the SisterSong Reproductive Health Collective in the 1990s, describes an approach to reproductive health that acknowledges the role of misogyny, racism and classism in reproductive oppression.

3-MINUTE SPEECH
The most influential work on reproductive justice was produced by two groups, SisterSong and Asian Communities for Social Justice (now called Forward Together). Both groups are still active in the US, running training programmes, workshops and media briefings on reproductive justice.

In 1994, the International Conference on Population and Development was held in Cairo, Egypt. After the conference, a group of women of colour met to discuss the issues they and other marginalized groups faced in relation to reproductive rights. Frustrated that abortion was the dominant issue in the reproductive rights movement, they coined the term 'reproductive justice' as a way to expand the discussion. One of the groups that emerged from this work was the SisterSong Collective, who defined reproductive justice as 'reproductive health integrated into social justice'. Abortion gives women the right not to have children. But historically, poor and minority women have been denied the right to have children. For example, there is a history in some countries of forcibly sterilizing poor and minority women, and in Canada, the USA and Australia of removing First Nations, Native American and Aboriginal children from their families for 'assimilation' into white culture. Reproductive justice has been an influential concept due to its holistic and radical political framing of reproduction as a human rights issue that extends beyond the right to abortion. It recognizes that reproductive oppression is based on gender, race and class, and that many women still face conditions that prevent them and their families from thriving.

3-SECOND BIOGRAPHIES
LORETTA ROSS
1953–
Reproductive justice activist and founder of the SisterSong Women of Colour Reproductive Justice Collective.

SYLVIA ESTRADA CLAUDIO
1957–
Filipina scholar of gender and reproduction who co-founded Likhaan, which works with grassroots women on issues of reproductive and sexual health and rights in the Philippines.

30-SECOND TEXT
Gillian Love

SisterSong turned the concept of reproductive justice into a human rights movement.

SISTERHOOD

black feminism Aims to empower black women with new and critical ways of thinking that centre on how racism and sexism create social issues and inequalities. Its theories show how race is gendered and gender is racialized.

capitalism Economic system based on private ownership of industry and trade for profit.

cis People whose gender identity matches the gender of their birth.

consciousness-raising The sharing of stories about women's lives and their experiences of sexual harassment, rape, abortion, domestic violence and sexist comments and stereotypes.

gendered Describes how an experience is affected by the gender of the subject, or how something particularly affects people differently based on their gender.

heteronormativity The political, social and cultural legitimization and privileging of heterosexual relationships and traditional gender roles as 'natural'.

heteropatriarchy The combination of heteronormativity and patriarchy.

heterosexism Discrimination against LGBTQI people and assumption that opposite-sex relationships and sexuality are the norm.

homophobia Dislike or prejudice against people who are lesbian, gay or bisexual.

imperial feminism Provides white Western feminists with institutionalized privilege that is founded upon inequality and exploitation and forges a feminism of asymmetrical power relations.

Lavender Menace Lesbian radical feminist group formed in 1970 which spoke out about the self-defeating hypocrisy of discriminating against women in a movement that claimed to champion sisterhood, and sparked lesbian activism in the feminist movement.

LGBTQI Umbrella term for the lesbian, gay, bisexual, transgender, questioning/queer, and intersex community..

patriarchal society The systematic dominance of men over women in all aspects of society.

politicize To make something political or to make someone politically aware.

queer Umbrella term to describe sexual and gender minorities who are neither heterosexual nor cisgender.

queer theory Seeks to eliminate heteronormativity by arguing that gender identity and gender roles are malleable, variable, social constructs.

racialize Make racial in tone or character; categorize or divide according to race.

Radicalesbians Formed by members of the Lavender Menace in 1970, their theories, including woman-identified-woman, had a major impact on politicizing feminism.

second-wave feminism Another way of referring to the women's liberation movement, which followed the 'first wave' (suffrage campaigns).

sexism Prejudice or discrimination based on sex or gender, especially against women and girls.

sisterhood Connotes a determination to work together in solidarity, as equals against male oppression.

Third World feminism Feminism that originates from internal Third World ideologies and socio-cultural factors, rather than being imported from the West.

transfeminism Movement by and for trans women who view their liberation to be intrinsically linked to the liberation of all women.

transnational feminism Contemporary movement that focuses on how globalization and capitalism affect people across nations, races, genders, classes and sexualities.

woman-identified-woman This term came out of lesbian activism during the women's liberation movement and referred to a woman who chose to organize her life around women rather than men.

women of colour (WOC) Political term used to collectively describe females of colour; emerged in the violence against women movement and became a unifying term in the 1970s for all minority women experiencing marginalization, with race and ethnicity as a common factor.

women's liberation movement (WLM) Explosion of feminist activism and theory from the 1960s–1980s. The name drew links with other movements, such as the black liberation movement.

WHOSE SISTERHOOD?

30-second feminism

3-SECOND SLAM
'Sisterhood' connotes a determination to work together as equals and a shared experience of male oppression.

3-MINUTE SPEECH
Robin Morgan edited two more books in the Sisterhood series, *Sisterhood is Global* (1984) and *Sisterhood is Forever* (2003), both comprehensive works about the women's movement. The notion of a feminist sisterhood paved the way for an indispensable collection of anthologies about solidarity by women from all over the world, such as Nigerian Obioma Nnaemeka's *Sisterhood, Feminisms & Power* (1998) and *Women Writing Resistance: Essays on Latin America and the Caribbean* (2017).

By the end of the 1960s, the women's liberation movement had radically affected relationships between women and men at large. This was its intention, of course. However, the movement failed to foresee that it would also transform the relationships that women had with one another. In 1968, radical feminist Kathie Sarachild coined the slogan 'Sisterhood is Powerful', which would become one of the three key catchphrases of second-wave feminism, alongside 'the personal is political' and 'consciousness-raising'. Writer and activist Robin Morgan popularized the phrase 'Sisterhood is Powerful' in her 1970 anthology of the same name. The anthology became an entry point into feminism for thousands of women and went on to be listed as 'one of the hundred most influential books of the twentieth century' by the New York Public Library. The book's central message was one of female solidarity, but considering that only three of the anthology's 57 articles were written by black women, it was an unbalanced message from the onset. As the concept spread, the more women of different race, sexuality, class and age backgrounds contested the power imbalance in feminist sisterhood. More often than not, however, the tension provided opportunity for more honest dialogue.

RELATED TEXTS
See also
WOMEN'S LIBERATION MOVEMENT
page 18

WOMANISM
page 20

THE FEMININE MYSTIQUE
page 60

3-SECOND BIOGRAPHY
ROBIN MORGAN
1941–
Writer and activist whose journalism and anthologies about sisterhood are essential feminist works; also author of poetry and fiction.

30-SECOND TEXT
Minna Salami

Notions of female solidarity – or sisterhood – have been fraught with issues of representation.

LAVENDER MENACE

30-second feminism

RELATED TEXTS
See also
STRANDS OF THEORETICAL
FEMINISM
page 26

THE FEMININE MYSTIQUE
page 60

HETEROSEXISM
page 110

3-SECOND BIOGRAPHIES
BETTY FRIEDAN
1921–2006
Author of *The Feminine Mystique*, attributed with starting second-wave feminism and founder of the National Organization of Women (NOW).

RITA MAE BROWN
1944–
Contributor to the Lavender Menace and bestselling author of over 40 books.

30-SECOND TEXT
Minna Salami

3-SECOND SLAM
The feminist movement owes much of its success to the radical perspectives brought to it by lesbians, but it also has a history of homophobia.

3-MINUTE SPEECH
The members of Lavender Menace later formed a group called Radicalesbians, whose theories had a major impact on politicizing feminism. One of their major contributions was the notion of the 'woman-identified-woman', which connotes a woman who organizes her life around women, rather than men.

On a late spring day in 1970, hundreds of feminists gathered to network and listen to presentations at the Second Congress to Unite Women in New York. In the middle of the programme, the auditorium lights suddenly went off. When they came back on, 20 women stood in front of the audience with the words 'Lavender Menace' printed across their T-shirts. They were members of a newly formed lesbian radical feminist group, whose name was a response to a homophobic remark made by feminist icon Betty Friedan, who in the heyday of second-wave feminism complained that lesbians were a 'lavender menace' who would potentially hurt the feminist cause. As everybody settled back in their seats, the Lavender Menace activists spoke about the self-defeating hypocrisy of discriminating against women in a movement that claimed to champion sisterhood. Yet, when they asked that those audience members who agreed with their cause join them in the front of the room, only a dozen women came forward. The impact that lesbians would come to have on the feminist movement, however, began to emerge the very next day, when Lavender Menace workshops filled to full capacity. Later, lesbians would produce some of the most critical theory about women's liberation, without which the sisterhood would be impoverished.

Lesbian activists have been a driving force in the feminist movement since the emergence of the Lavender Menace.

THIS BRIDGE CALLED MY BACK (1981)

30-second feminism

3-SECOND SLAM
A foundational text of the modern feminist movement, *This Bridge Called My Back* enabled women of colour to express their voices in an unprecedented way.

3-MINUTE SPEECH
This Bridge was part of a US Third World Feminism inspired by the Third World Women's Alliance (TWWA), which sought to create ideological and political links with people of colour in Africa, Latin America and Asia in order to bring the revolution home through an antisexist, antiracist and anti-imperialist agenda.

For women of colour (WOC), the notion of sisterhood was fraught with difficulties from the beginning. Although white feminists, who coined the slogan 'Sisterhood is Powerful', may have condemned racial discrimination in society, they rarely tried to bridge the gap within the movement. That effort – to bridge the gap of power imbalance due to racial and ethnic differences – was relegated to WOC. In the aptly titled 1981 anthology *This Bridge Called My Back*, edited by Cherríe L. Moraga and Gloria E. Anzaldúa, Asian, African-American, Latina and Native American women expressed their experiences of prejudice and denial of differences within the feminist movement. They challenged the naïve sentiment implied in the term 'sisterhood', namely that women were a homogenous group dealing with patriarchy in identical ways. *This Bridge* was not merely a reaction against racism in the white feminist movement, it was a project of solidarity, reflecting what it meant to be a radical WOC feminist. It also dealt with topics such as divisions within WOC and explored Third World Women's writings 'as a tool for self-preservation and revolution'. The anthology was a revolution in style, combining prose, poetry, critique, personal narrative, fiction, spirituality and art in a way that came to define feminist writing.

RELATED TEXTS
See also
WOMANISM
page 20

WOMEN IN INDEPENDENCE MOVEMENTS
page 52

INTERSECTIONALITY
page 72

3-SECOND BIOGRAPHIES
GLORIA E. ANZALDÚA
1942–2004
Poet, metaphysical philosopher and scholar of Chicana cultural theory, feminist theory and queer theory.

CHERRÍE L. MORAGA
1952–
Poet, playwright, cultural activist and author of many influential books.

30-SECOND TEXT
Minna Salami

The anthology This Bridge Called My Back *became a game-changing text of the movement.*

18 February 1934
Born in Harlem, New York, of a Grenadian mother and Barbadian father

1954
Spends a year at the National University of Mexico, which she remembered as 'a time of affirmation and renewal'

1961–68
Works as a librarian in New York public schools

1968
Publishes her first volume of poems, *The First Cities*

1978
Diagnosed with breast cancer and undergoes a mastectomy

1980
Founds Kitchen Table: Women of Color Press with Barbara Smith, who publish, among other books, *This Bridge Called My Back*

1982
Publishes what she refers to as her 'biomythography': *Zami – A New Spelling of My Name*

1984
Publishes the widely read essay collection *Sister Outsider* and moves to Berlin, Germany, becoming influential in Afro-German liberation

17 November 1992
Dies in her home in Saint Croix, the Virgin Islands, from liver cancer

AUDRE LORDE

Audre Lorde was (in her own words) a black lesbian feminist. She was careful to label herself this way because, as she once put it, 'I'm not one piece of myself. I cannot be simply a black person, and not be a woman too. Nor can I be a woman without being a lesbian.'

Perhaps her need to express the different parts of her identity stemmed from having grown up in 1940s Harlem, a place where race had a sorrowful impact on young Audre's life but where she, in an otherwise loving home, was not allowed to express her sorrow, as she describes in her memoirs.

Her experiences drew her to becoming a poet, activist and thinker whose rich body of work remains a go-to for anyone who seeks a deep understanding of oppression and liberation, and the processes in between the two, especially as they relate to race, gender, sexuality and class. Few thinkers have been able to fill the gap of candid and incisive writing that Lorde left, which greatly enriched the women's movement.

The longevity of Lorde's work owes not only to her polemical, passionate and prophetic views of social issues: her impact lasts also because of the way that she ties together poetry with theory, the intellect with the emotions, and the individual with the community, creating a new, fluid language to contrast with old, rigid ways of thinking.

Feminist sisterhood was of great importance to Lorde, but she was clear that solidarity was not easy work. In one of her best-known essays 'Your Silence Will Not Protect You', written just after receiving chemotherapy for breast cancer, Lorde famously addressed a group of white feminists, saying: 'The fact that we are here and that I speak these words is an attempt to break that silence and bridge some of those differences between us, for it is not difference which immobilizes us, but silence. And there are so many silences to be broken.'

In the 1980s, Lorde moved to Berlin where she became a leader in the Afro-German women's movement. In 1987, she moved to Saint Croix in the Virgin Islands, where she also became involved in women's liberation. Wherever Lorde went, she helped people discuss their sorrows concerning racism, sexism, homophobia and class division in ways that not only politicized them but also made them feel hopeful.

Lorde wrote nine poetry collections, five books of prose and a fictionalized memoir called *Zami – A New Spelling of my Name* (1982). She died from cancer at home, at the age of 58.

Minna Salami

BLACK FEMINISM

30-second feminism

Black feminism originated from the need to fight back against how black women experienced sexual oppression in the black liberation movement and how they experienced racial oppression in the feminist movement. Formally, black feminism was cemented with the 1973 founding of the National Black Feminist Organization in New York. Yet the black feminist tradition goes further back in history and beyond the US borders, which have nevertheless shaped the movement. Black feminists asked questions such as: How does race and/or class affect a woman's life in patriarchal society? Which issues directly impact women of different backgrounds? By probing into questions about how race, class and gender intersect, black feminists developed theory that showed how race is gendered and gender is racialized. That is, they showed how all too often 'black' was equated with black men and 'woman' was equated with white women. One of the central texts of black feminism is the 'Combahee River Collective's Feminist Statement', written in 1974. The statement argued that racism, sexism, capitalism and heterosexism are all branches of a singular oppressive structure and must therefore be challenged simultaneously in order to challenge any single one of them.

3-SECOND SLAM
Any analysis of feminism-at-large would be incomplete without considering black feminism, which brought to the fore the ways that race, class and gender are intertwined.

3-MINUTE SPEECH
The feminist movement and the antiracism movement have always grown in tandem. The first wave of feminism in the nineteenth century emerged out of the anti-slavery movement, and the second-wave women's liberation movement has its origins in black and Third World liberation movements, hence the use of the term 'liberation'.

RELATED TEXTS
See also
WOMANISM
page 20

INTERSECTIONALITY
page 72

HETEROSEXISM
page 110

3-SECOND BIOGRAPHIES
BEVERLY GUY-SHEFTALL
1946–
Pioneer of Black Women's Studies who has often addressed the negative reaction to feminism in the African-American community.

BARBARA SMITH
1946–
Author, activist and a writer of the 'Combahee River Collective Statement'; co-founded Kitchen Table, the first US publisher of women of colour, and nominated for a 2005 Nobel Peace Prize.

30-SECOND TEXT
Minna Salami

Black feminism seeks to represent the true meaning and experience of being a black woman.

IMPERIAL FEMINISM

30-second feminism

3-SECOND SLAM
Due to the global power order, feminists of white, Western heritage are dominant within the movement and this has negative consequences.

3-MINUTE SPEECH
As well as having to deal with the effects of foreign and indigenous patriarchies, feminists in the developing world are forced to resist yet another layer of oppression caused by imperial feminism – a skewed focus on narratives of oppression and factors such as poverty, female genital mutilation, prostitution, disease and war in the depiction of women's lives outside of the West.

If you scan through the global pool of women's resistance, you are left with the impression that challenging patriarchy is of predominant interest to white, Western women. The world's most-known feminist activists, such as Elizabeth Cady Stanton, Emmeline Pankhurst and Simone de Beauvoir, first come to mind when naming influential feminists. This is not simply because white, Western feminists have contributed to the movement in important ways, but it is also due to the relationship between patriarchal and imperialist power structures. These power structures have had devastating effects on women in the Global South. Imperialism is the control of one territory by another through economic, military or ideological means, and women especially suffer under foreign control. Imperial feminism is a term applied to those who champion women's rights and yet support imperialism, despite the negative effects it has on women's lives beyond the West and ultimately on Western women themselves through the strengthening of patriarchies. Early British feminists such as Emmeline Pankhurst endorsed the Empire, arguing it was a means to 'remove and destroy ignorance'. Such legacies still manifest in our times, with 'feminist' rhetoric being used to justify war or to assert control over women's bodies in the name of population control.

RELATED TEXTS
See also
POSTCOLONIAL FEMINISM
page 28

GLOBAL FEMINISM
page 38

FEMINISM & INTERNATIONAL LAW
page 54

3-SECOND BIOGRAPHY
CHANDRA TALPADE MOHANTY
1955–
Professor, writer and one of the first feminists from the developing world to strongly criticize imperial feminism; argued in *Under Western Eyes* that white and Western feminisms 'appropriate and colonize' the lives of women in developing countries.

30-SECOND TEXT
Minna Salami

Imperial feminism propagates the myth that 'other' women need saving by white Western 'saviours'.

QUEERING FEMINISM

30-second feminism

3-SECOND SLAM
Despite an initial tension
between queer theory and
feminist theory, each has
been influenced, and
strengthened, by the other.

3-MINUTE SPEECH
In the almost three decades
since *Gender Trouble* was
published, a significant
amount of people have
rejected heteronormative
gender identities and
identify instead as 'queer'.
The term 'queer' can be
used as an umbrella term to
refer to all LGBTQI people,
but it can be – and often is
– merely used as a political
statement to indicate an
anti-heteronormative and
alternative lifestyle that
advocates fluidity in
sexual orientation and
gender identity.

In 1990, the highly influential if
notoriously abstract classic book *Gender Trouble*,
by Judith Butler, was published. By arguing that
gender identity and gender roles are malleable
social constructs, the book provided a shattering
critique of 'heteronormativity' – the political,
social and cultural legitimization and privileging
of heterosexual relationships and traditional
gender roles as 'natural'. Conversely, by critiquing
heteronormativity it also discombobulated
the heteronormative position that other forms
of relationships and gender identities are
'unnatural', or queer. Queer theory has its roots
in Butler's book, among others. In the early
stages especially, there was a tension between
queer theory and feminist theory. Queer theory
seeks to eliminate heteronormativity, while
feminist theory seeks to eliminate patriarchy.
Although the two are connected in what could
be referred to as 'heteropatriarchy', feminist
critiques of biological difference in shaping
womanhood clash with the idea that femaleness
and maleness are social – rather than biological
– constructs, as queer theory posits.

RELATED TEXTS
See also
THIRD WAVE
page 22

HETEROSEXISM
page 110

WHIPPING GIRL
page 132

3-SECOND BIOGRAPHY
JUDITH BUTLER
1956–
Writer and academic whose
work has made a significant
impact not only on feminist
thought and queer theory but
also on twenty-first century
intellectual thinking.

30-SECOND TEXT
Minna Salami

*Feminists argue that
heterosexuality is
constructed to maintain
male domination and
oppress women.*

WHIPPING GIRL (2007)

30-second feminism

3-SECOND SLAM
Whipping Girl was
a key work in making
transfeminism accessible
to a cisgender audience,
and demonstrating
how trans liberation
ties into traditional
feminist concerns.

3-MINUTE SPEECH
Transfeminism – of which
Whipping Girl is a part –
began in 1987 with Sandy
Stone's *The Empire Strikes
Back: A Posttransexual
Manifesto*, although the
term 'transfeminism' was
only defined in 1992 by
Diana Courvant. The field
strongly contrasts (by
necessity) with second-
wave feminism, starting
from a position that gender
and gendered experiences
are fundamentally relative.
In this respect it is
commonly associated with
intersectionality, and has
strong overlaps with
transnational feminism.

Trans people in general – and
transfeminine people in particular – have often
been treated as objects of derision or contempt
by wider society, and frequently cut out of
feminist movements. There is a particularly
long history in second-wave feminism of trans
women being seen as illegitimate, and not truly
being women (or experiencing womanhood).
In *Whipping Girl* (2007), Julia Serano drew upon
her background as a trans woman to articulate
the strong overlaps between transmisogyny
(misogyny experienced by transfeminine people)
and normative sexism. Deconstructing her
experiences of misogyny, Serano made the case
for trans liberation to be treated as a feminist
movement, and for trans concerns to be taken
up by traditional feminism. While *Whipping
Girl* was not the first transfeminist work, its
accessible tone and central premise that it
should be of interest to cis feminists brought
wider attention to the field. The frankness with
which Serano discussed and debunked many
myths about trans women – particularly around
medical transition, informed by her background
as a biologist – have made *Whipping Girl* a
frequent resource for members of the trans
community, particularly those who are newly
out to themselves, and for educating those
new to trans issues.

RELATED TEXTS
See also
THIRD WAVE
page 22

INTERSECTIONALITY
page 72

3-SECOND BIOGRAPHIES
SANDY STONE
1936–
Media theorist and artist,
Sandy Stone's *The Empire
Strikes Back: A Posttransexual
Manifesto* is considered
a foundational text of
Trans Studies.

JULIA SERANO
1967–
Gender theorist, trans rights
activist and biologist whose
books include *Whipping Girl*,
Outspoken and *Excluded*.

30-SECOND TEXT
Os Keyes

*Serano argues that
Western sexism
comprises both
traditional and
oppositional sexism.*

A MOVEMENT OF PROTEST

ableism Also known as disablism. Discrimination and prejudice against disabled people, particularly through harmful stereotyping and labelling practices.

activism Vigorous, direct campaigning to bring about social or political change.

authoritarianism An ordered and controlled political system that concentrates power in the hands of a leader or a small elite at the expense of individual freedoms.

civil rights Laws and legislature that protect individuals from unequal treatment based on certain protected characteristics (race, gender, disability, etc).

cultural activism Influences and creates art, books, film, music and theatre, and can change individual and societal attitudes by enabling the presentation of alternative viewpoints and allowing the questioning of dominant narratives.

democratic structuring Authority within an organization being distributed among as many people as possible and delegated for specific tasks, rotation of tasks, frequent diffusion of information to all and equal access to resources.

division of labour Separation of tasks to allow for and encourage specialization, particularly in an economic system or manufacturing, to maximize productivity and efficiency.

DIY punk movement Anti-consumerist self-sufficiency, empowering individuals and communities; linked to punk ideology.

guerrilla Used in feminist art and activism to talk about subversive actions taken intentionally, without seeking official approval or sanction, often anonymously; actions performed in an impromptu, unauthorized way.

heterosexism Discrimination against LGBTQI people and assumption that opposite-sex relationships and sexuality are the norm.

honour killing Murder of a person (usually a woman) accused of bringing shame upon their family and/or community, committed by those (usually a family collective) who perceive they are defending their reputation; often a result of strongly misogynistic views towards women.

human rights Basic rights and freedoms that belong to every person in the world, throughout their life, and include dignity, fairness, equality, respect and independence.

hypermasculinity The exaggeration of male stereotypical characteristics or behaviour, such as physical strength, aggression and sexuality; can be encouraged by a patriarchal society.

LGBTQI Lesbian, gay, bisexual, transgender, questioning/queer, intersex people.

marginalization Pushing a group or person to the fringes of society by treating them as insignificant, thereby restricting their influence or possible contribution to society.

patriarchy The systematic dominance of men over women. Men hold the power and dominate in roles of political leadership, moral authority, social privilege and control of property.

racism Belief that one race or ethnicity is superior over another. Patricia Bidol contended that racism occurs when prejudice is combined with institutional power.

sex strike Refusal (normally by women) to take part in sexual intercourse until certain goals are achieved.

sexism Prejudice or discrimination based on sex or gender, especially against women and girls.

sit-in protest Occupying a public space or business by means of peaceful protest; appropriated as a tactic by various rights' movements, such as the civil rights movement and feminism.

suffrage The right to vote in political/governmental elections.

totalitarianism The rule of the state over public and private life; power is dictatorial and leaders demand complete subservience; the most extreme and complete form of authoritarianism.

MOVEMENT TACTICS

30-second feminism

Feminist groups and activists use different tactics to achieve their goals. Activists engage in online and offline consciousness-raising, to bring more into the movement, develop common analysis and mobilize for action. They organize direct action, whether this is physical occupation of spaces, protests and rallies, escorting women to abortion clinics, or damaging the property of the oppressor or state. The refuge movement is one way in which groups provide services – in this instance, to women experiencing violence. Additionally, feminists seek to engage with power, as politicians, civil servants or in advocacy. They have engaged in writing and speaking, drawing on analysis developed by others while developing their own, to spread messages and develop feminist thinking. Cultural activism, with feminists making art, music, poetry and literature, or being active in the media, is also key to success, by shaping societal attitudes and behaviour. Indeed, many groups engage in a number of tactics, making decisions as to what will work and alliances with others using different strategies. Moreover, feminists are increasingly paying attention to ensure movement sustainability, whether this means self-care, engaging with younger women or mechanisms to resolve intra-movement conflict.

3-SECOND SLAM
Feminists use a diverse range of tactics, working together – and sometimes disagreeing – about which is the most appropriate and effective.

3-MINUTE SPEECH
Feminists can disagree on tactics and how outspoken and radical to be. For example, those fighting for suffrage in the UK were split on direct action, with suffragists and suffragettes taking opposing sides. While conflict can be healthy, it can split movements. Mutual accusations – for example, of caring about respectability, selling out, or damaging the movement by being 'too radical' – are worsened by denunciations from those resisting change.

RELATED TEXTS
See also
CONSCIOUSNESS-RAISING
page 62

REFUGE MOVEMENT
page 82

FEMINIST LEADERSHIP
page 146

30-SECOND TEXT
Chitra Nagarajan

Feminist thinking is constantly evolving on social media, in books and through activism.

ABA WOMEN'S WAR

30-second feminism

3-SECOND SLAM
Women in the old Aba region of Nigeria protest against unfair taxation – and win – in one of the first uprisings against British colonial power.

3-MINUTE SPEECH
Colonializing powers sought consciously to change societies in line with Victorian England gender norms to 'civilize natives' and 'save women'. They reinforced the authority of men at the expense of women, undermined structures of women's leadership and power, and reified binaries of man as provider and woman as homemaker. These actions have continued resonance today, as these gender roles have become internalized in many societies as expressions of 'tradition' and 'culture'.

In the late nineteenth century in Nigeria, British colonizing officials ruled through appointed warrant chiefs, replacing more egalitarian systems. Colonial and local elite men became increasingly oppressive and corrupt, imprisoning critics, forcing labour and confiscating women's animals and profits. Women, previously playing important roles in political and economic governance, were marginalized and became frustrated, staging protest dances and songs in Calabar province in 1925. The last straw was taxing women contrary to previous practice, including on cooking pots, utensils and clothing. Calling upon traditional practices of women's protest, the women of Okolo town, led by Ikonnia, Nwannedia, Nwanyereuwa and Nwugo, invited others to join them. Actions included women of different ethnicities and spread to surrounding areas, across 6,000 miles-squared, from November to December 1929. They staged nightlong song and dance ridicule to censure men, blocked roads, destroyed warrant chief and colonial powers' property, but caused no physical human harm. Soldiers shot and killed unarmed protesters and burned villages as collective punishment, but the Aba women forced authorities to drop taxation plans, remove warrant chiefs and put in place a new governance system.

RELATED TEXTS
See also
WOMEN IN INDEPENDENCE MOVEMENTS
page 52

FEMINIST ECONOMICS
page 74

IMPERIAL FEMINISM
page 128

3-SECOND BIOGRAPHIES
IKONNIA, NWANNEDIA & NWUGO
fl. 1910–30
Women of Okolo who led the women's war, known for their powers of persuasion, intelligence and passion, respectively.

NWANYEREUWA
fl. 1920–30
Widow living in Okolo, whose anger at attempts to tax her property sparked discussions that led to the start of the protest.

30-SECOND TEXT
Chitra Nagarajan

The Aba women inspired further protests in the 1930s–1950s.

MEMOIRS FROM THE WOMEN'S PRISON (1983)

30-second feminism

3-SECOND SLAM
Jailed for alleged 'crimes against the state', Nawal el Sa'adawi tells the story of her months with other political prisoners in the women's prison.

3-MINUTE SPEECH
Women who defend human rights, including those of women, face the same risks as men, such as surveillance, unfair trials, torture and assassination. They also face additional threats, such as sexual and domestic violence, attacks against their reputation, conviction of 'moral' crimes and threats against families, because they are women. Perpetrators can be government officials, security agents, community leaders and even the women's own families and male colleagues.

Amidst internal unrest, President Sadat of Egypt arrested many opponents and critics in 1981. Among them was Nawal el Sa'adawi, a leading activist, feminist, socialist, doctor and writer. The author of *Woman at Point Zero, The Hidden Face of Eve* and *Woman and Sex*, books exploring honour killings, sexual abuse, female genital mutilation and women's subjugation, she had been dismissed from the Ministry of Health for her writing in 1972. In her 1983 book *Memoirs from the Women's Prison*, she narrates from the moment the police knocked on her door to her visit of those still in prison after her release. A classic of prison writing, the book charts her thoughts and observations of fellow prisoners, a diverse range of Marxists, intellectuals, Islamist conservatives and fundamentalists. Written on toilet paper in prison and completed afterwards, its evocative prose conveys the disorientation of being jailed with no information as to why. It shows the brutality of prison and lack of even pretence of justice, as well as the kindness, community and alliances among women prisoners to maintain mental health, obtain better conditions and resist state violence. Despite later censorship and death threats, el Sada'awi published almost 50 books and plays, ran for the presidency and participated in the 2011 pro-democracy protests.

RELATED TEXTS
See also
POSTCOLONIAL FEMINISM
page 28

INTERSECTIONALITY
page 72

3-SECOND BIOGRAPHIES
NAZRA FOR FEMINIST STUDIES
est. 2007
Egyptian feminist organization that supports women's rights.

WOMEN HUMAN RIGHTS DEFENDERS COALITION
est. 2008
Network that supports and protects women human rights defenders worldwide.

HARASSMAP
est. 2010
Volunteer-based initiative that reports and maps sexual harassment to support offline community mobilization.

30-SECOND TEXT
Chitra Nagarajan

In 2008 Nawal el Sa'adawi won a case brought by Al Azhar University accusing her of apostasy and heresy.

1989
Puncture magazine publishes 'Woman, Sex and Rock and Roll', the first manifesto of the movement

1990
Punk musicians Allison Wolfe and Molly Neuman publish the first issue of the zine *Girl Germs*

1991
'Your Dream Girl', the first radio programme to address young women, hosted by Lois Maffeo, debuts on KAOS, a radio station in Washington state. Around 50 bands perform over six days of the International Pop Underground Convention, focused on artists' DIY ethic and taking over the means of production

1991
Molly Neuman, together with musicians Allison Wolfe, Kathleen Hanna and Tobi Vail, publish a new zine called *Riot Grrrl*. Musicians come together in a benefit concert called Rock for Choice, to show support for the pro-choice movement and women's rights, with subsequent concerts held in dozens of cities across the US and Canada until 2001

1992
Erika Rienstien and May Summer found the Riot Grrrl Press as a zine archive and distribution network

1992
Media outlets mischaracterize riot grrrl and start applying the term to any women-fronted rock band, regardless of their politics, leading many in the movement to speak out

2000
Over 2,000 people attend the first Ladyfest, a DIY community-based festival for feminist and women artists, bands and poets, which is then adapted and spread by women across the world from Amsterdam to Shanghai

2014
Many of riot grrrl bands, such as Sleater Kinney, Bratmobile and L7, reform, release new albums or announce tour dates

RIOT GRRRL

In 1980s United States, men dominated rock and punk music scenes. Women had to fight to 'earn' their place in the mosh pit, and commonly experienced groping and other violence. The riot grrrl movement claimed women's space, combining feminist analysis with DIY punk politics. The riot grrrl Manifesto (1991) started with, 'BECAUSE us girls crave records and books and fanzines that speak to US that WE feel included in and can understand in our own ways.' Bands such as Bikini Kill, Bratmobile, Heavens to Betsy, L7, Le Tigre, Sleater Kinney and The Slits directly challenged sexism with their music talking about violence, sexuality, racism and women's empowerment, and requiring men to move to the back in concerts so women could be at the front.

Young women came together in 'chapters' around Canada, Europe and the US. They merged art and activism through direct political action, music and zines – short magazines, produced by one person or a small group of people, with limited circulation. Feminist zine culture became the latest in a long history of women's self-publication, allowing women to write and spread ideas otherwise unpublished. The writing, sharing and reading of zines by thousands of girls and young women merged the personal and political in discussions of their lived experiences and issues such as violence, abortion, body image and sexuality.

Young women also gathered in local meetings, national conferences and grassroots organizing to protect abortion rights, focus on violence against women and protest the treatment of Anita Hill, who testified before the Senate about her sexual harassment by Supreme Court nominee Clarence Thomas. Although it tried to be diverse, riot grrrl has been criticized for consisting of mostly middle-class white girls and women.

Inevitably, riot grrrl was not only attacked and denigrated by male fans and musicians but also misrepresented, distorted and ridiculed by mainstream media. By the mid 1990s, its radical message had been co-opted by the music industry and women-centred and girl-power bands. Most of the bands split, but many of the women involved still make political music.

While zines live on in print, blogs and sites such as Tumblr, riot grrrl's continued impact can be seen on a generation of women artists, musicians and music journalists. Festivals like Ladyfest and the Girls Rock camps, where girls aged 8–18 years old are taught by older women musicians to play instruments, form bands and perform shows, continue to bring women together in the same feminist and DIY ethic.

Chitra Nagarajan

Group portrait of riot grrrl group Voodoo Queens, London, 1992.

FEMINIST LEADERSHIP

30-second feminism

Feminist activism has often been associated in the public eye with specific movement leaders. Yet feminism critiques patriarchal models of leadership and styles involving hierarchies, division of labour, differential value attached to different work and power based on dominance and authority. Indeed, it has a strong critique of the very idea of leaders, with many groups trying to have flatter, more democratic processes and/or operating as collectives. In doing so, they aim to share power and improve the skills of all members while building communities of support and resistance. This can be difficult. Conflict within the movement can be more emotionally taxing than that elsewhere, often with a greater sense of betrayal, and political differences getting personal very quickly. Meanwhile, in the workplace, feminist leaders challenge hierarchies, making power visible, democratic, legitimate and accountable at all levels, working towards flatter power structures and making decisions collaboratively and through consensus-building. Feminist leaders strive to make everyone feel respected and valued; build inclusive, diverse, collaborative and positive spaces; emphasize empathy; and act to challenge sexism, racism, ableism, heterosexism and other marginalization. They mentor and empower colleagues.

3-SECOND SLAM

Feminism challenges power hierarchies and patriarchal leadership models, both in feminist and other organizing, and in the workplace.

3-MINUTE SPEECH

Many groups resist having leaders as non-democratic, concentrating power and valuing certain people and work over others. However, when groups lack any structure, 'structurelessness' masks who holds power, with rules of how decisions are made known only to a few. Jo Freeman argues instead for democratic structuring, with authority distributed among as many people as possible and delegated for specific tasks, rotation of tasks, frequent diffusion of information to all and equal access to resources.

RELATED TEXTS

See also
CONSCIOUSNESS-RAISING
page 62

INTERSECTIONALITY
page 72

MOVEMENT TACTICS
page 138

3-SECOND BIOGRAPHIES

JO FREEMAN
1945–
Civil rights and feminist activist, lawyer, political scientist and author of 'The Tyranny of Structurelessness'.

CREA
est. 2000
Indian feminist human-rights organization that strengthens feminist leadership for social transformation.

JASS
est. 2003
Global women-led human-rights network.

30-SECOND TEXT
Chitra Nagarajan

Feminist leaders care about well-being, build community and balance work and family life.

LIBERIA WOMEN'S MASS ACTION FOR PEACE

30-second feminism

Between 1989 and 2003,

Liberia's civil wars killed an estimated 200,000–250,000 people and displaced a further 1.5 million. Tired of the violence, women from different walks of life, led by Leymah Gbowee, Asatu Bah Kenneth and others, came together. They announced that women would go on sex strike until war ended. Thousands of women dressed in white staged sit-in protests along routes taken by President Charles Taylor and opposition fighters, and persuaded them to attend peace negotiations in Ghana. Women then shuttled between delegates to negotiate positions. While weeks dragged by and warlords jockeyed for power, violence escalated. The women grew increasingly worried. They barricaded the doors of the negotiating hall, threatened to strip naked in protest and gave delegates two weeks to agree a peace deal – or they would act again. A peace agreement was signed two weeks later. Afterwards, the women worked with child soldiers, urged fighters to give up weapons and campaigned in elections for Ellen Johnson Sirleaf, who became the first female African president. The mass action ended two-and-a-half years after it had begun, with the women vowing to step back up if their country needed them again.

3-SECOND SLAM
Thousands of women from different backgrounds helped end the 14-year Liberian Civil War, forcing warring parties to negotiate and sustain peace through non-violent protest.

3-MINUTE SPEECH
Feminist analysis sees how the machinery of war requires hypermasculine men to fight and 'vulnerable' women to protect. Many women fighting for suffrage were anti-war. Women are integral to movements against nuclear weapons, the arms race and forced conscription. Thousands of women protested between 2010 and 2011 to end the Côte d'Ivoire civil war. In conflicts from the former Yugoslavia and Israel/ Palestine to Northern Ireland, women have cooperated for peace across lines of division.

RELATED TEXTS
See also
WOMEN IN INDEPENDENCE MOVEMENTS
page 52

THE MOTHERS OF THE PLAZA DE MAYO
page 104

ABA WOMEN'S WAR
page 140

3-SECOND BIOGRAPHIES
LEYMAH ROBERTA GBOWEE
1972–
One of the leaders of the movement, awarded the 2011 Novel Peace Prize; co-founder of the Women in Peace and Security Network.

ASATU BAH KENNETH
fl. 2000–
Founder of the Liberian Muslim Women's Organization, part of the mass action, who reshaped the police to take women's security more seriously.

30-SECOND TEXT
Chitra Nagarajan

Women involved in the mass action were commended for their non-violent efforts to build peace.

PUSSY RIOT

30-second feminism

The feminism of Pussy Riot, formed in Russia in 2011, focuses on how authoritarian regimes reinforce gender norms and intrinsically opposes totalitarianism. Members combine challenging discriminatory policies – including restrictions on abortion and support for LGBTQI rights – with critique of President Vladimir Putin's regime. Arguing only vivid illegal actions bring media attention and subsequent public debate, they stage unauthorized guerrilla performances in public spaces, including churches, the underground, luxury stores, next to a prison holding opposition activists and in Red Square. Videos of performances and their songs are posted online, free to download. Lyrics range from urging the Virgin Mary to become a feminist and support them in their protests, through calling for Russians to protest elections likely to be rigged by throwing cobblestones during street clashes, to opposing police brutality and corruption in the criminal justice system. In 2012, three members were arrested and convicted of hooliganism, motivated by religious hatred for performances in churches which criticized Russians' subservience to the Church, the Church's traditionalist views on women and the Church leaders' support for Putin.

3-SECOND SLAM
Russian feminist punk collective that stages performances challenging authoritarianism, religious conservatism and economic inequality, and calls for fulfilment of civil, political and economic rights.

3-MINUTE SPEECH
Nadezhda Tolokonnikova, a Pussy Riot member, has said their performances are dissident art or political action that engages art forms. Cultural activism influences and creates art, books, film, music and theatre, and can change individual and societal attitudes. It enables the presentation of alternative viewpoints, allows people to question dominant narratives and becomes part of what feminist publisher and thinker Bibi Bakare-Yusuf calls the archive of the future, that which is known by future generations.

RELATED TEXTS
See also
MOVEMENT TACTICS
page 138

#FEMINISM
page 152

3-SECOND BIOGRAPHIES
YEKATERINA SAMUTSEVICH,
MARIA ALYOKHINA &
NADEZHDA TOLOKONNIKOVA
1982–, 1988–, 1989–
Convicted of hooliganism for their performance critiquing the Orthodox Church's anti-feminist ideology and links to Vladimir Putin.

PYOTR VERZILOV,
OLGA PAKHTUSOVA,
OLGA KURACHYOVA &
VERONIKA NIKULSHINA
1987, 1992–, 1993–, 1997–
Ran onto the pitch during the 2018 World Cup final as a protest against the state.

30-SECOND TEXT
Chitra Nagarajan

The cases against Pussy Riot have brought global condemnation, from governments to human rights activists.

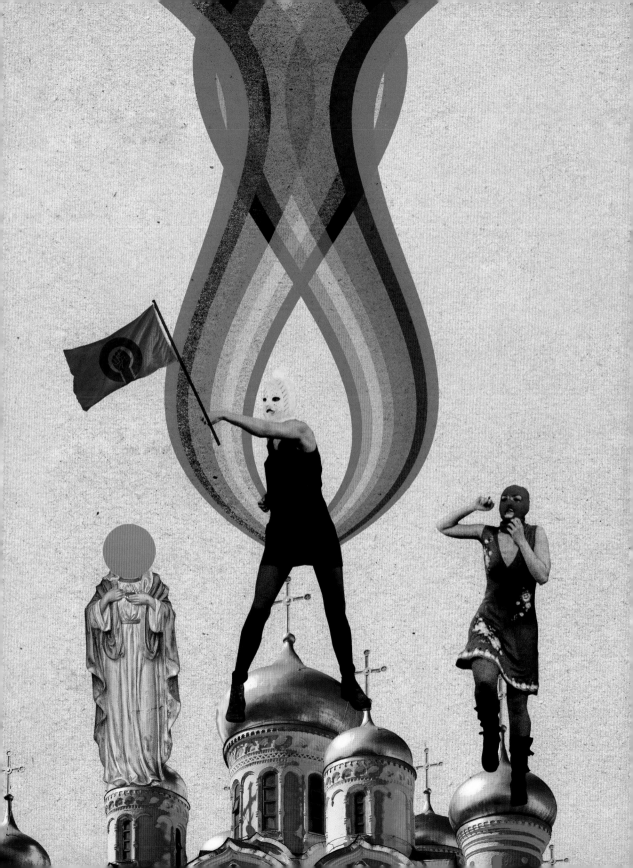

#FEMINISM

30-second feminism

Cyber stalking. Rape and death

threats. Sharing intimate images without consent. The Internet is used to intimidate, humiliate and control women and girls. Yet activists are working to #imagineafeministinternet, where more feminists and queer people are involved in making decisions and technologies, and the Internet is not run by a handful of corporations. Online spaces are used to challenge patriarchy and violence in a form of consciousness-raising for the digital age, using hashtags such as #EverydaySexism and #BeingFemaleinNigeria. In 2015, Brazilian feminists launched #MeuPrimeiroAssedio (#MyFirstHarassment). Women shared experiences, online and offline, leading to street protests in several Central and South American countries. In 2017, #MeToo, the name of a campaign run by Tarana Burke since 2005, was used by women to share experiences of sexual violence, causing several powerful men to lose their jobs and sparking global conversations. For example, China's Ministry of Education pledged to implement policies to prevent harassment, and legislators discussed amending the country's Civil Code. There are critiques that these hashtags centre on elite women, but social media has also provided many opportunities to talk and learn about intersectionality, through hashtags such as #GirlsLikeUs.

3-SECOND SLAM
As our lives increasingly merge online and offline, the Internet is a site of violence as well as activism, resistance and movement building.

3-MINUTE SPEECH
Surveillance by governments and others, rights to privacy, digital security and control over data are feminist issues. A feminist Internet takes agency and consent seriously. Women must be able to make informed decisions about what information about them will be online and available to others, particularly given how technology can be used to monitor women, restrict their rights and threaten women human rights defenders.

RELATED TEXTS
See also
THE RISE OF ONLINE FEMINISM
page 32

CONSCIOUSNESS-RAISING
page 62

INTERSECTIONALITY
page 72

3-SECOND BIOGRAPHIES
TAKE BACK THE TECH
est. 2006
Global campaign that highlights and acts against tech-related violence against women and girls.

FEMINIST PRINCIPLES OF THE INTERNET
est. 2014
Developed by activists from six continents to bring a gender and sexual rights lens on Internet rights.

30-SECOND TEXT
Chitra Nagarajan

Online feminist activity is contributing to a more representative and accountable Internet – and society.

RESOURCES

MOVEMENTS & WEBSITES

Bitch Media
BitchMedia.org

Blackfeminisms.com

Digital Feminism
digitalfeminism.co.uk

Domestic Worker's Bill of Rights
https://labor.ny.gov/legal/domestic-workers-bill-of-rights.shtm

Feminist Principles of the Internet
feministinternet.org

Feministing
feministing.com

Finally Feminism 101
finallyfeminism101.wordpress.com

Genderqueer.me

Grassroots Feminism
www.grassrootsfeminism.net

International Civil Society Action Network
www.icanpeacework.org

Ms. Magazine
msmagazine.com

National Organization of Women (NOW)
now.org

National Woman's Party (NWP)
www.nationalwomansparty.org

National Women's Hall of Fame
www.womenofthehall.org

Rise Up!
riseupfeministarchive.ca

Take Back the Tech
www.takebackthetech.net

The Body is Not an Apology (TBINAA)
thebodyisnotanapology.com

The Everyday Sexism Project
everydaysexism.com

Women Human Rights Defenders Coalition
www.defendingwomen-defendingrights.org

Women in Black
womeninblack.org

Women's International League for
Peace and Freedom
wilpf.org

Women's Media Center
www.womensmediacenter.com

BOOKS & ESSAYS

Ain't I A Woman
bell hooks
(Pluto Press, 1987)

African Sexualities
ed. Sylvia Tamale
(Pambazuka Press, 2015)

Black Feminist Thought
Patricia Hill Collins
(Routledge, 2008)

Black on Both Sides: A Racial History of Trans Identity
C. Riley Snorton
(University Of Minnesota Press, 2017)

Encyclopedia of Gender and Society
ed. Jodi O'Brien
(SAGE Inc., 2009)

Everyday Sexism
Laura Bates
(Simon & Schuster, 2014)

Feminism Without Borders
Chandra Talpade Mohanty
(Duke University Press Books, 2003)

In Her Own Right: The Life of Elizabeth Cady Stanton
Elisabeth Griffith
(Oxford University Press, USA, 1985)

Invisible Lives: The Erasure of Transsexual and Transgendered People
Viviane K. Namaste
(University of Chicago Press, 2000)

Not that Bad
Roxane Gay
(Harper Perennial, 2018)

Pornography
Andrea Dworkin
(The Women's Press Ltd, 1981)

Queer African Reader
ed. Sokari Ekine and Hakima Abbas
(Pambazuka Press, 2013)

Revolting Prostitutes: The Fight for Sex Worker's Rights
Molly Smith & Juno Mac
(Verso Books, 2018)

Sexual Politics
Kate Millett
(Virago, 1977)

The Body is Not an Apology
Sonya Renee Taylor
(Berrett-Koehler, 2018)

The Cause
Ray Strachey
(Virago, 1978)

RESOURCES (cont.)

The Feminist Revolution
Bonnie J. Morris and D-M Withers
(Smithsonian Books, 2018)

'The Tyranny of Structurelessness'
Jo Freeman
www.jofreeman.com/joreen/tyranny.htm

Trans Kids
Tey Meadow
(University of California Press, 2018)

Transgender History
Susan Stryker
(Seal Press, 2017)

Understanding Trans Health
Ruth Pearce
(Policy Press, 2018)

Women Against Fundamentalism
ed. Sukhwant Dhaliwal & Nira Yuval-Davis
(Lawrence & Wishart, 2014)

Yes Means Yes
Jaclyn Friedman
(Avalon Publishing Group, 2008)

Yes, You Are Trans Enough
Mia Violet
(Jessica Kingsley Publishers, 2018)

NOTES ON CONTRIBUTORS

EDITOR
Jess McCabe is the former editor, now editor-at-large, of feminist website *The F-Word*, recognized as a globally powerful force in millennial feminist thought. She is an award-winning journalist reporting on gender issues, sustainability and housing, writing for *The Guardian*, *Women's eNews* and *Bitch* magazine. McCabe was named IBP Journalist of the Year in 2013 and Feature Writer of the Year in 2018.

CONTRIBUTORS
Veronica I. Arreola is a professional feminist, writer and parent. She is an expert on diversity in science and engineering.

Laura Bates is an English feminist activist and writer. She founded the Everyday Sexism Project in 2012, and is the author of *Everyday Sexism, Girl Up* and *The Burning*.

Red Chidgey is Lecturer in Gender and Media at King's College London. She is the author of the book *Feminist Afterlives* (Palgrave, 2018).

Shannon Harvey got her first taste of feminist campaigning when she won the right to wear jeans like the boys to the Sunday school picnic. Her feminism has been evolving ever since, including through a career that started in domestic violence services in London and now sees her raising funds for reproductive justice in New York City.

Os Keyes is a PhD student at the University of Washington, studying gender, data, infrastructure and control, and is an inaugural Ada Lovelace Fellow. They can be found at: https://ironholds.org.

Gillian Love is a feminist researcher whose work focuses on abortion in the UK. She was awarded her PhD from the University of Sussex, where she currently teaches Sociology and Gender Studies and writes about women's experiences of ending pregnancies.

Nadia Mehdi works broadly within the traditions of feminist philosophy and philosophy of race. She teaches at both the university and schools level with the University of Sheffield in the UK. Her current research focuses on oppression and resistance at our cultural peripheries.

Chitra Nagarajan is an activist, researcher and writer who works on human rights and building peace, and is involved in feminist, anti-racist, anti-fundamentalist and queer movements. She is part of the editorial collective of 'Feminist Dissent', an academic journal focused on gender and fundamentalism, and co-editor of *She Called Me Woman: Nigeria's Queer Women Speak*.

Minna Salami is a writer, critic and speaker, and the founder of the award-winning blog MsAfropolitan, which connects feminism with critical reflections on contemporary culture from an Africa-centred perspective. She is a contributor to *The Guardian*, CNN and BBC, as well as a speaker for the EU and the UN. Her debut book, *Sensuous Knowledge*, is forthcoming in 2020.

Sarah Tobias is Associate Director of the Institute for Research on Women at Rutgers University and an affiliate faculty member in the Women's and Gender Studies Department. She has a PhD in Political Science from Columbia University (USA) and an undergraduate degree in History from Cambridge University (UK).

INDEX

ACKNOWLEDGEMENTS

EDITOR'S ACKNOWLEDGEMENTS
With great thanks to Chitra Nagarajan, Jennifer Pozner and Helen G., whose ideas and input helped shape the contents of this book.

PICTURE CREDITS
The publisher would like to thank the following for permission to reproduce copyright material on the following pages:

Alamy/ClassicStock: 61C; Dino Fracchia: 19C, 81TC; Everett Collection Historical: 61T (L–R); Historic Images: 141B; ITAR-TASS News Agency: 151 C&CR; Keystone Press: 81B; The Picture Art Collection: 45B, 53CL; Pictures Now: 61BL; RosalreneBetancourt 10: 104; ZUMA Press, Inc.: 50.

Dreamstime/Donpat: 141BG.

Getty Images/Corbis Historical: 121C; David Degner: 143C; DEA Picture Library: 45TR; Hannelore Foerster: 34; Hulton Deutsch: 83C; Jack Mitchell: 124; Jean-Claude FRANCOLON: 93C; John Minihan: 83B; Martyn Goodacre: 144; PIUS UTOMI EKPEI: 149B; Sunset Boulevard: 65C; Teenie Harris Archive/Carnegie Museum of Art: 119CL; William Foley: 84.

Library of Congress, Washington D.C. 9BGC, 9C, 17BGC, 17C, 37CR, 47TR, 47CR, 49CR, 49CL, 63C (main images), 63B, 73TL, 73BL, 73BR, 91CR, 91C, 99B, 119BR, 123BG,123TC, 123CL, 129B; /Historic American Buildings Survey: 47BG; /Fred Palumbo: 61BR.

Peter H. Raven Library/Missouri Botanical Garden: 101C.

The Royal Łazienki Museum/Andrzej Ring: 55C (main image).

Shutterstock/005th: 83BG; 3dpic: 29TC; 7Crafts: 2C, 39C; Africa Studio: 83BG; Ahturner: 107CR; Akin Ozcan: 111TR; alexandre zveiger: 153B; Alexandros Michailidis: 29T, 127CR; Alex Leo: 153TR; Alex Volot: 101C; Algol: 31BC; AlisaNata: 119TC; Amelia Fox: 109CT; Andrey Eremin: 63CL; Angel Soler Gollonet: 25BGC; Annmarie Young: 21BG; Anton Watman: 61BC; ArtaKM: 37CLT; Artush: 61CL; Arun Benjamin Christensen: 75TR; Asier Romero: 113BC; Asymme3: 63CR; Avivi Aharon: 89CR; aykutkoc: 31C; Axel Bueckert: 127BG; Billion Photos: 21CL&R; Brett Allen: 23BGC; Byelikova Oksana: 19T; Cactus Studio: 121C(logo); Cagkan Sayin: 61CL; chanafoto: 65CR; Chekmareva Irina: 27BL; Christian Bertrand: 23C; Christina Li: 107C; Claudio Divizia: 113TCR(moon); Cory Seamer: 89BC; Crazy nook: 25TR; cristi 180884: 99C; Darrin Henry: 123CR; David Carillet: 25TL; David M. Schrader: 101B; Denis Kuvaev: 109TL; Designs Stock: 109CR; Digital Storm: 27CR; Dja65: 67BG; Dmitriy Maiorescu: 133BC; doddis77: 23BGT; durantelallera: 6C, 89BC, 139C; Elena Ray: 119CR; Eleonora_os: 109C; Ensuper: 29C, 31B; EPG_EuroPhotoGraphics: 127B; ESB Professional: 2CR, 39CR, 87TR; Everett Collection: 19CR, 25C, 25BC, 27L, 27C, 27R, 33BC, 37B, 37BGT, 37CL, 55LC, 65TR, 65TL, 71BR, 71C, 73BC, 73TC, 73TR, 75TR, 81C, 87C, 93BC, 99C,101CL, 101CR, 119BL, 131C, 133C; Everett Historical: 9BGT, 9BGL, 17BGT, 17BGL, 31C, 45TL, 47C, 47CL, 49C, 103BL, 103BR; Expensive: 25CT; Fabian Plock: 149CL; fixer00: 101TBG; Flashon Studio: 113TR; Fosin: 133CL, 133CR; Galyna_P: 19BGT; Gelpi: 103C; Gencho Petkov: 67BG; German Nareklishvili: 29TCR, 29TCL; GSK919: 75TC; gladder: 149TL; graphixmania: 87CBG; grebeshkovmaxim: 131C; GreenBelka: 127T; g-stockstudio: 55CR; hans. slegers: 81TL; IgorGoloniov: 91BL; Image Flow: 25TR; Imageman: 99TC; India Picture: 2CR, 39CR, 113C; Irina Levitskaya: 89C; Istvan Csak: 81CR; iunewind: 27C; ixpert: 153C (globe); Jacob Lund: 6BR, 67CT, 139BR; Janusz Pienkowski: 53CR; javarman: 33BGT; Jemastock: 151T; john dory: 127C; John Gomez: 29CL; jorisvo: 103C; jumpingsack: 65TL; Kathy Hutchins: 68; Ken Wolter: 89TBG; Krafted: 33TC; Ksenija Toyechkina: 2BG, 39BG; lev radin: 153C, 39CL, 55L(R); Ljupco Smokovski: 2CL, 39CL, 55L(R); Lucian Coman: 103CR; lynea: 131T; Lyudmila2509: 19BC; Meranda19: 109CR; MJTH: 111C; michaelheim: 6BC, 139BL; michaeljung: 2C, 2BC, 2BL, 39C, 39BC, 39BL, 87TL, 107CR; 107BR, 113TL; Michael Steden: 63CL; Mina Tepes: 55L; Morphart Creation: 119BG; mrwebhoney: 153CR; Naypong Studio: 67CL, 67CR; Neirfy: 23B; Neo Tribbiani: 47TL; New Africa: 21T, 127CL, 143C; nexus 7: 81TR; nobeastsofierce: 143BGT; NY-P: 65BL; oksana2010: 65CL; Olena Boronchuk: 21B, 121TC; oriontrail: 111BG; OSTILL is Franck Camhi: 33BC, 109TR; Ozaiachin: 25BG; PAKULA PIOTR: 71BL; patpitchaya: 67BG; pernsanitfoto: 153BG; photka: 153B; Photomontage: 27CL; PILart: 107B; Prostock-studio: 153B; PT Images: 21C; Radha Design: 131C; Raevsky Lab: 6TC, 139TC; Ramona Heim: 103C; Rashad Ashur: 63TR; Ratchawoot: 33B; Rawpixel. com: 11, 147 (outer hands), 153B; Richard van der Gpuy: 6BC, 139BC; Rich Koele: 75BG; Rob Leyland: 89CL; RODINA OLENA: 31BGC; rook76: 9BGC, 17BGC; Sabphoto: 27BG; Samuel Borges Photography: 6CL, 81CL, 139CL; sanjagrujic: 67C; Sergei Bachlakov: 29BR; Sergey Ogaryov: 153TR; SF photo: 121BGC; Shams Suleymanova: 101BL, 101BR; sirtravelalot: 103B; SoRad: 11C, 147C; Spaskov: 107BC; staras: 67BC; Stas Malyarevsky: 19BGC; Stefan Nielsen: 151B; Stocksnapper: 49T; studiovin: 61CR; Sunflowerr: 25TL; SvetlanaFedoseyeva: 109CB; szefei: 55CL, 55L, 107CL, 113BR; takayuki: 107CL; Tanya Syrytsyna: 63T; the palms: 101C; trekandshoot: 61CL; Vector Posters and Cards: 61CR; Victoria 'Tori' Meyer: 113BG; Viktoria Bykova: 111T; Voin_Sveta: 131B, 133BC; wavebreakmedia: 55CT, 107TC; Webicon: 103TL, 103TR; Wlad74: 27B; wong sze yuen: 2CBR, 39CBR; xiaorui: 67BR; xmee: 93BC; xpixel: 107BG; Yes - Royalty Free: 87TBG; Yuriy Boyko: 55BG; Zastolskiy Victor: 19BGC; Zoltan Katona: 141BGT; Zovteva: 31CR, 31CL; zydesign: 23TC.

Wellcome Collection/CC BY 4.0: 53B.

Wikimedia Commons/Internet Archive Book Images: 99BG; Rod Waddington: 129C; Schmidt Kunstauktionen: 47B.

All reasonable efforts have been made to trace copyright holders and to obtain their permission for the use of copyright material. The publisher apologizes for any errors or omissions in the list above and will gratefully incorporate any corrections in future reprints if notified.